Advanced Charting
Technical Analysis

1 Candlestick Formations

1.) How do we use Candlesticks?

There are significant differences between how we use candlesticks and how most techniques do. The creation of candlesticks as indications to enter positions is given significant weight, as is the case with many methods. Candlesticks are just another TOOL for us to be able to forecast and enter at the most likely times, as we have already touched on. Numerous candlestick formations help us time entries so that we can enter at the best price while increasing the probability of our setups. The many forms we're about to examine are ones you'll see repeatedly because they aid with entry, management, and exit.

High Test

high test

high test

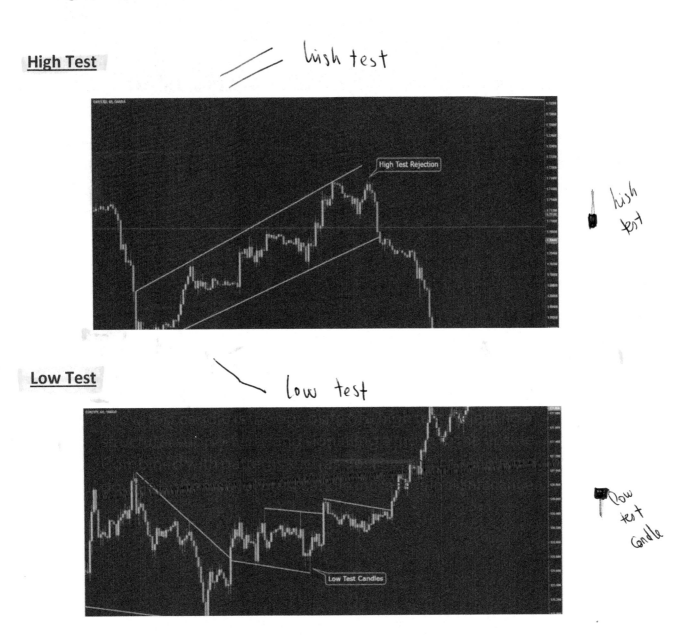

Low Test

low test

low test candle

Doji

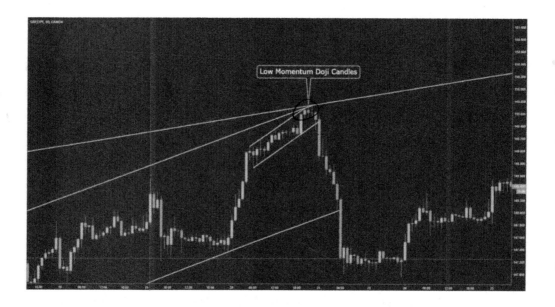

A low momentum candle known as a doji closes exactly where it began and hasn't moved very far in either direction. Doji candles are most common when there is a price slowdown, which is typically after the correction of an impulsive move, as it approaches a structural support level, or continuously during the corrective phase as price slowly moves sideways. We learn that there is a slowing of momentum when the doji candle appears numerous times in a row, which helps us better comprehend price behavior.

Bullish Engulfing

(moving up)

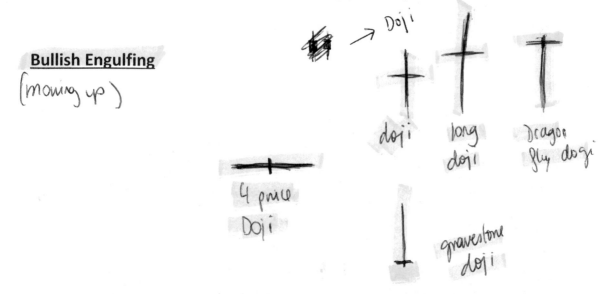

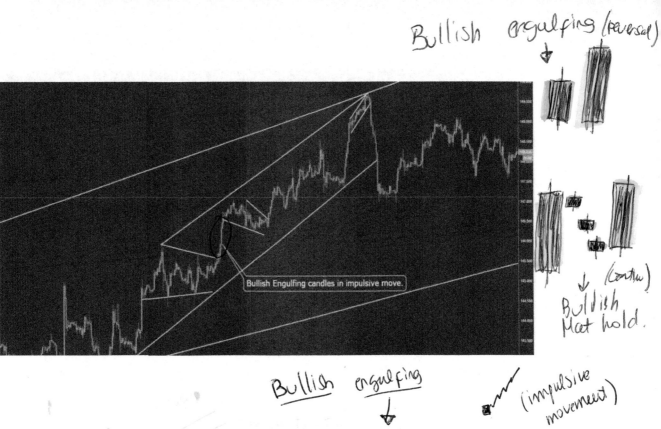

Bullish engulfing (reversal)

Bullish engulfing
↓
(continu.)
Bullish Mat hold.

Bullish engulfing
↓

(impulsive movement)

Bullish Engulfing candles in impulsive move.

An **engulfing** candle that is bullish indicates upward movement. Bullish engulfing candles are used to determine whether price is moving impulsively or correctly.

Candlesticks are one of several tools we use to identify the market's stage, but they are an important one.

Bearish Engulfing (moving down)

Reversal

Continuation

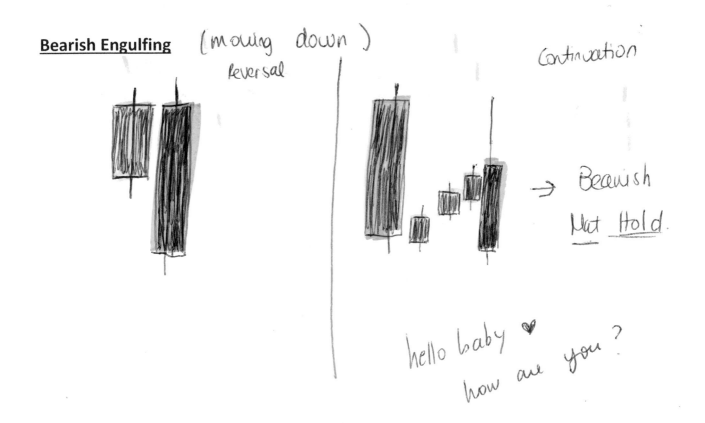

→ Bearish Mat Hold.

hello baby ♥ how are you?

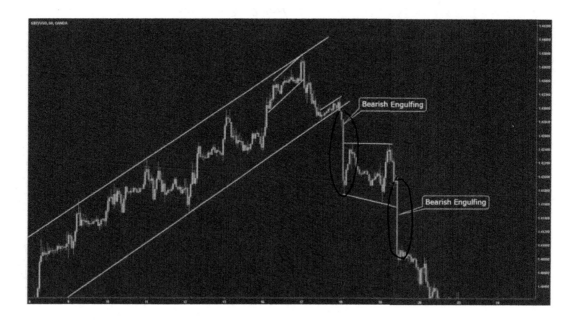

A bearish engulfing candle has momentum that is moving downward. In the impulsive legs of selling opportunities, we witness bearish engulfing candles. When the market starts to gain momentum and a pair starts to decline, bearish engulfing candles

→ bearish engulfing to decline.

1hr Retrace

We frequently use the 1H Retrace candle as an entry point for the majority of the trades we enter because it is a very potent candlestick formation. It simply represents the rejection of a defined region by fully retracing the preceding candle and, depending on whether it was a buy or sell, closing above or below where the initial candle opened.

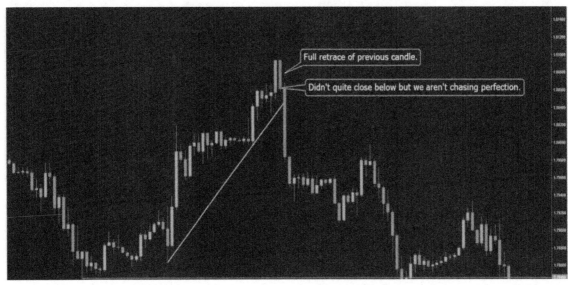

Full retrace of previous candle.

Didn't quite close below but we aren't chasing perfection.

1h retrace ▮▮

Evening Star

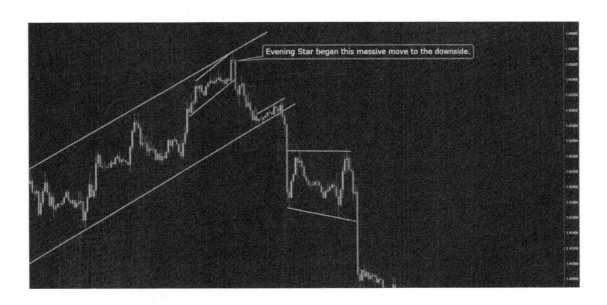

Evening Star began this massive move to the downside.

This candlestick formation is not as frequent as some of the others that you may repeatedly encounter. However, there is a difference when you do see a clear

Evening stars, particularly on longer time scales, can be a very excellent sign that strong momentum is about to begin. The evening star shows a bullish engulfing, a doji, a bearish engulfing that is around the same size as the first bullish engulfing candle, and finally a bearish engulfing.

┃ + ┃

evening star (bearish)

Morning Star

Morning star.

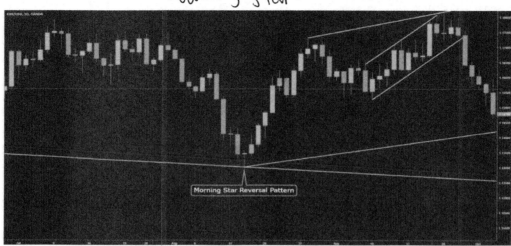

Similar to the evening star, the morning star is not a candlestick formation that frequently appears (less frequently than the evening star), but when it does, it is a strong entry point and, if present on the higher time frames, it is a signal that you may start to see weekly or monthly moves play out (when combined with other forms of analysis). As the example below does not show a complete retracement of the first candle, they are not always perfectly formed, but as was already mentioned, we are not chasing perfection but rather a signal that the trade is likely to reverse.

→ *morning star (bullish)*

Hanging Man

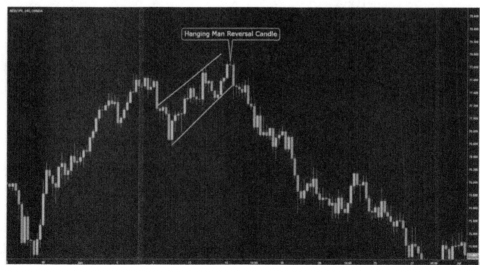

Though it will be located in a different area, it is very similar to a low-test candle.

→ *hanging man (market is losing momentum.)*

It is typically viewed as a reversal type candle since it occurs at the end of an exhausted run when the market is losing momentum. This candle is found at the top of a run rather than rejecting the bottom of a structural region despite having a long lower wick.

The only physical difference is where you locate it; everything else is the same.

Tweezer Tops

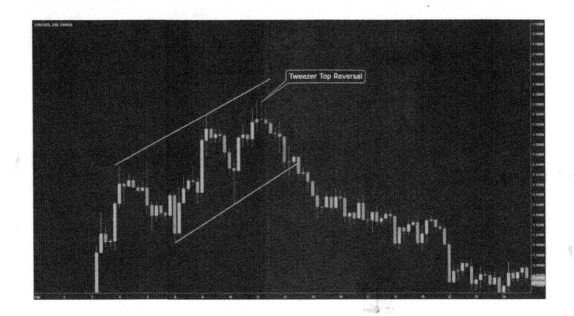

Two high test candles placed back-to-back in this arrangement signify a twofold rejection of the region in which they occur. Price probed a region over the course of two complete formations before closing back down just before the candle's opening. It is more potent than a single high test and frequently indicates that the price is about to decline.

Tweezer Bottoms

reversal.

(Bearish)

(2 high test back to back - tweezer tops, which means price is about to drop.

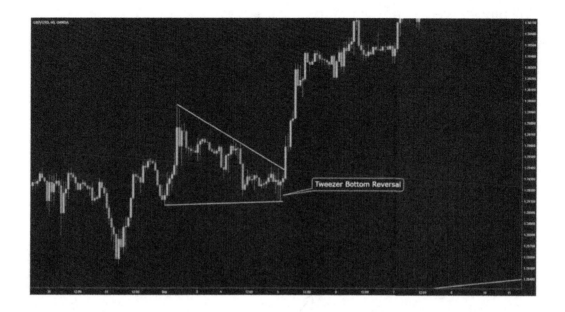

Two low test candles that are back-to-back in this pattern signify a twofold rejection of the region in which they appear. Price probed a region over the course of two complete formations before closing back down just before the candle's opening. It is frequently an indication that pricing is about to move higher and is more potent than a single low test.

→ tweezer bottom

(bullish)

(indication that pricing is about to move higher more potent than a single low-test.

What Is Market Structure?

In its most basic form, structure is the process of using trend lines and ray lines in charting software to build a "framework" for the market over a number of timeframes based on the natural laws that govern how the market functions and moves. This framework helps us understand and interpret what is happening. We use the aforementioned data across all timeframes (Month, Week, Day, Half Year, and Year) to understand market sentiment and, as a result, create a bias that enables us to profit from bullish and bearish moves by

foreseeing the timing of both and the path of the subsequent market breathing cycle.

Market structure → process of using trend lines to build a "framework" → forecast over a number of times buxd on how the market moves.

has a different forecast

The price action has an outside framework that has been painted upon it, as seen from an HTF perspective. On lower time frame charts, the inner structure exhibits its own behavior and price movement. We'll go into more detail about the Entry Types to help you better understand price action.

Risk Entry

framework

risk entry as its above the framework.

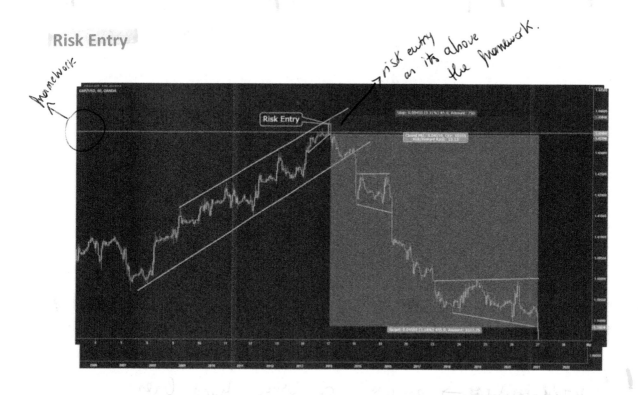

Risk Entry

Reduced Risk Entry

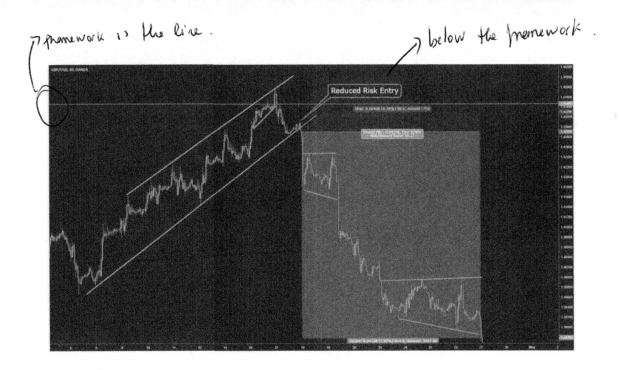

Patterns

Reversal Patterns

<u>Ascending Channel</u>

ascending channel/rising

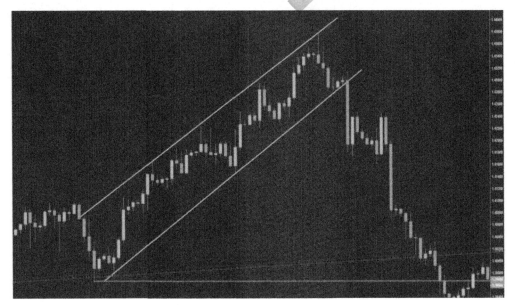

An inversion patterns that we frequently observe in our analysis is a rising channel. They are obvious at all times, and we can spot them by observing whether or not the market has a quick or remedial idea

Descending Channel

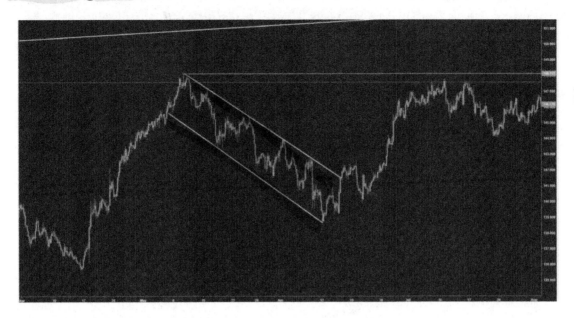

Two downward trendlines drawn above and below a price, which represent resistance and support levels, combine to form a descending channel on a chart.

The term "falling channel" or "channel down" are other names for the descending channel pattern.

(A Rising Wedge)

Drawing two ascending trend lines, one for highs and one for lows, results in a

chart pattern called a rising wedge. In addition to rising to the right, the upper line has a steeper slope than the lower trend line.

Typically, a rising wedge has three reversals for one trend line and two for the opposing trend line, for a total of at least five reversals.

Falling Wedge

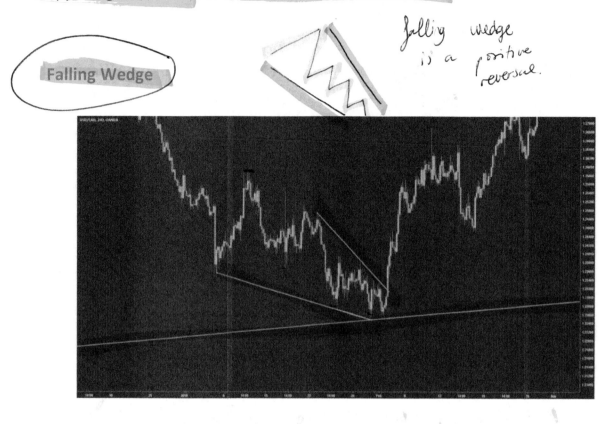

falling wedge is a positive reversal.

Drawing two descending trend lines, one to represent the highs and one to represent the lows, results in a chart pattern known as a falling wedge. It is classified as a chart pattern with a positive reversal.

Head And Shoulder

Center

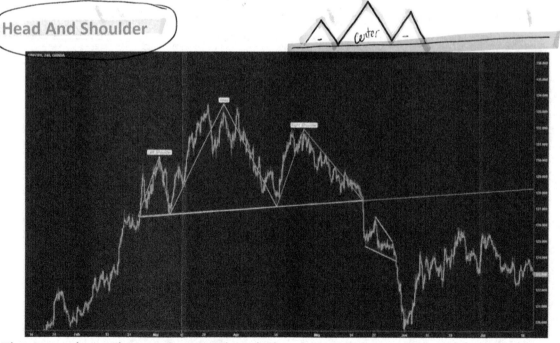

Three peaks make up the Head and Shoulders chart pattern; the centre peak is the tallest, with the outside two peaks being quite similar in height.

Inverse Head And Shoulder

A reversal chart pattern known as a "Head and Shoulders Bottom" is an inverse head and shoulders.

The Head and Shoulders pattern is comparable, except this one is inverted.

With the centre low ("head") being the deepest and the two outside lows ("shoulders") being shallower, the pattern consists of three sequential lows.

The two shoulders should have an ideal ratio of height to width.

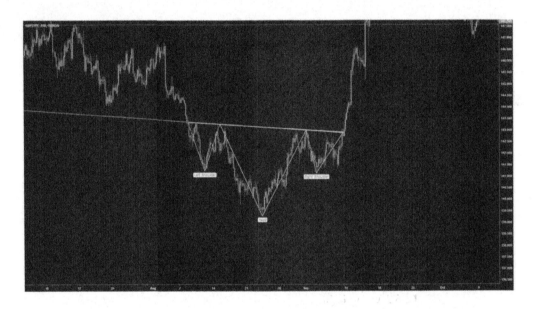

Double Top

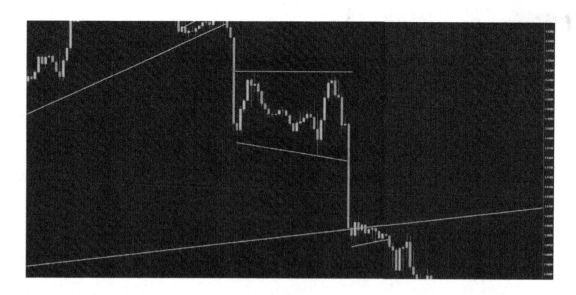

Double Bottom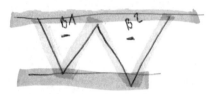

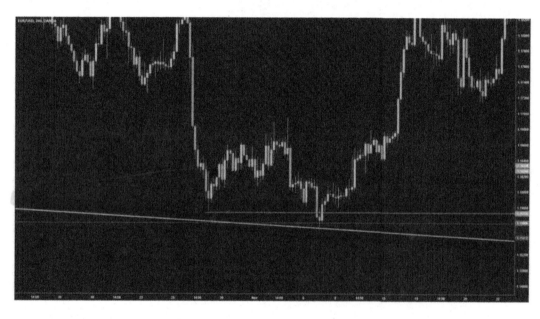

Continuation Patterns

Bull Flag

Bear Flag

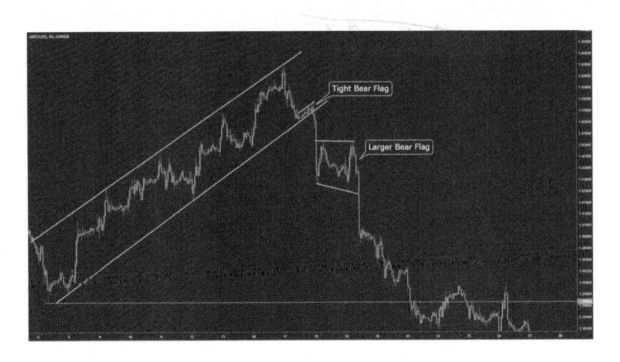

Flat Continuation

Symmetric Triangle

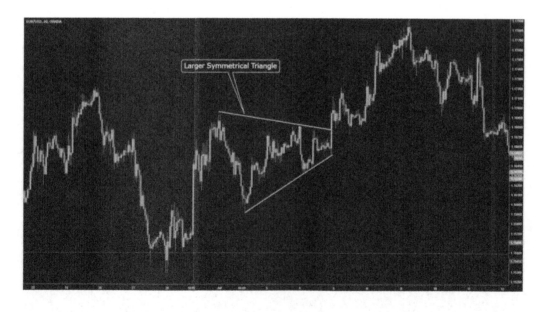

Another form of continuation we might order as we study price action is a balanced triangle. It appears as though a banner is being 'pressed' or crushed out of its shape. The more money is incorporated into the banner's improvement, the more we may begin to classify it as an example of a particular type. This allows us to designate the region of the example where a gamble or a reduced risk passage is most likely to occur.

Expanding Triangle

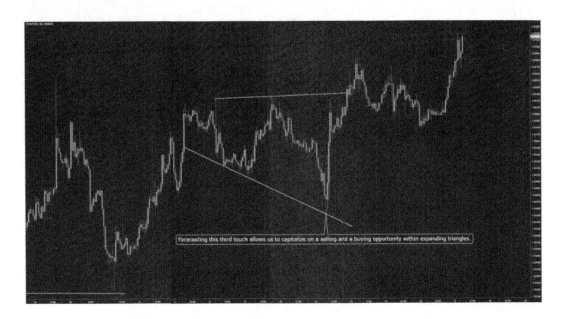

Forecasting this third touch allows us to capitalize on a selling and a buying opportunity within expanding triangles.

Multi-Touch Confirmations

We may now change the range of abilities with additional support to stack positions in our favor because we are continually extending our understanding of how to analyze price action and have thoroughly practiced various aspects of the approach. The best topic to discuss after patterns is multi-touch confirmation because it adds another factor to take into account that might increase the likelihood of a trade.

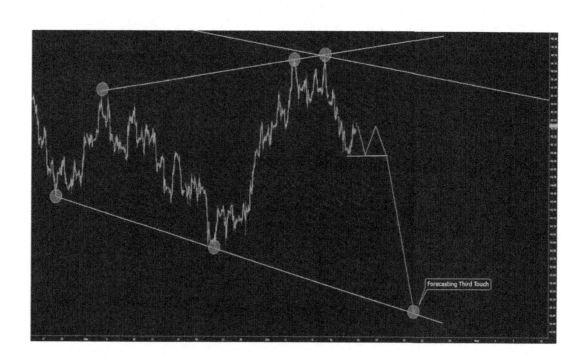

Forecasting Third Touch

MARKET STRUCTURE, PRICE ACTION AND TECHNICAL ANALYIS 2.0

The structural underpinnings of the trading tactics you will learn about in the next chapters will be thoroughly covered in this chapter. We will examine the fundamental components of market movement and discover the two fundamental elements—impulses and corrections—that underpin all price moves. Here, we'll establish the groundwork for comprehending market movements and the distinctive patterns they leave in their wake. The significance of accurately identifying price structures, the ramifications and complications of using various time frames, and the discovery of a straightforward, five-part classification system that would catalog every conceivable type of price change are all covered in great depth. The information offered here must be subconsciously absorbed in order for it to serve as the foundation for the five trade setups you will learn later. As a result, I advise reading this chapter slowly and going over each subject as many times as necessary to thoroughly understand it. The outcomes you obtain as a trader will directly correlate with how well you internalize the material presented here, so take it seriously and take your time.

Fundamental versus technical analysis

There are two schools of thought that can be used to comprehend and predict price changes in the financial markets: fundamental analysis and technical analysis. While the focus of this book and your subsequent work will be primarily on the latter strategy, let's examine each one separately, starting with fundamental analysis.

Fundamental Analysis

Fundamental analysis attempts to comprehend all of the factors that could influence the relative balance of supply and demand for a particular stock, currency pair, or commodity in order to establish an assessment of value through careful examination of financial statements, economic reports, marketplace competition, and earnings statements. Fundamental analysis places a lot of emphasis on mathematical models that take into account the importance of these aspects in an effort to forecast what the price of a financial asset should be in the future. Although this approach is sound in theory, it has a significant flaw: it rarely, if ever, takes other market participants into account, one of the most significant factors that influence price movement. The people who actively purchase and sell financial assets are what move markets, not beautiful mathematical models, whether these participants are hedge funds, financial institutions, or individual traders like me. A basic evaluation could accurately weigh the importance of any number of factors, leading to a reasonable projection and value assumption. However, it has little significance if the traders and speculators, who are largely responsible for the majority of the trading volume, are purchasing and disposing of that asset based on a different expression of value. In actuality, many short-term traders have little understanding of the fundamental forces that are thought to influence prices and base the majority of their trading decisions on variables that are wholly unrelated to the purportedly logical fundamental models. I'm not fully dismissing fundamental analysis in any way; I'm only trying to make the point that it's not very useful for short-term trading, hence the focus of this book.

Technical Analysis

The study of historical price changes is known as technical analysis. We can identify quantifiable patterns that repeat with a high degree of regularity and statistical reliability by focusing on the actual price changes and, consequently, the actions that led to them. Technical analysis ignores all underlying factors that "could" affect price and instead concentrates on the actuality of price, organizing the collective actions of the people driving these price changes into profit-generating trading opportunities. Markets are actually influenced by a wide range of factors that are nearly hard to accurately quantify. With the aid of technical analysis, we are able to stand back and base our trading decisions on the outcome of all those market-moving variables. Charts, a graphical representation of price movement over time, are used in technical analysis. Important hints about the underlying purchasing and selling pressure can be found on a chart.

Technical analysis and chart reading are neither singularly correct or one method. While some technical traders prefer to trade trends using straightforward price patterns, others place a strong emphasis on numerical technical indicators. By the end of this chapter, you will be familiar with the technical framework I employ and the supporting tools, both of which have a long history of successful use.

TA1.0 and TA2.0

In the past, simple chart patterns and, more recently, the use of complex technical indicators have dominated technical analysis (TA). This technical analysis is version 1.0. Trading based solely on the price's position in reference to historical levels, reinforced by secondary indicators, lacks one important piece of information: HOW it arrived at that precise level or developed that certain pattern. Simple pattern recognition just provides you with a one-dimensional understanding of the market, excluding the more complex nuances of price action and market structure. Although it is possible to trade by merely recognizing price patterns, this method greatly undervalues the richness and depth of understanding that come with having more sophisticated technical proficiency.

Consider the rookie trader's typical learning curve. Most technical traders will first become familiar with many chart patterns, numerous candlestick formations, and even hundreds or even thousands of indicators that are accessible in most contemporary charting software. The same trader, however, soon comes to the realization that there is a growing disconnect between his level of expertise and his actual bottom-line trading performance. This is TA 1.0's problem. It concentrates on one straightforward topic: knowing when to purchase and sell. The plethora of signs and patterns still fall short of providing the trader with even a fundamental grasp of why markets behave the way they do. The nature of price changes is not attempted to be understood. Herein lies the value of TA 2.0..

Technical Analysis 2.0

technical examination The next stage of technical trading is 2.0. Charts are maintained as clean as possible, focusing attention on market structure and price activity across a range of time frames. They are based on clarity and consistency. The charts are not messed up by secondary or auxiliary indicators that produce ambiguous or conflicting indications. Instead of employing price derivatives, trades are made using price itself as the indicator. When studying market structure, emphasis is put more on the process by which price generated a pattern or structure than on the structure itself.

Take TA 1.0 signals from support and resistance levels as an example. In TA 1.0, the trader would recognize areas of support and resistance, or points where there is a strong likelihood that the price will turn around. The trader would normally go long after identifying a resistance zone if the price rose above the level since it was believed that the buyers had overcome any overhead barrier and were likely to continue rising further. This is where TA 1.0 falls short. The location of the price is the only focus; its origin is less important. What if price broke the same resistance level in the shape of an ascending channel, a pattern with a high propensity to function as a reversal pattern? The following graph illustrates.

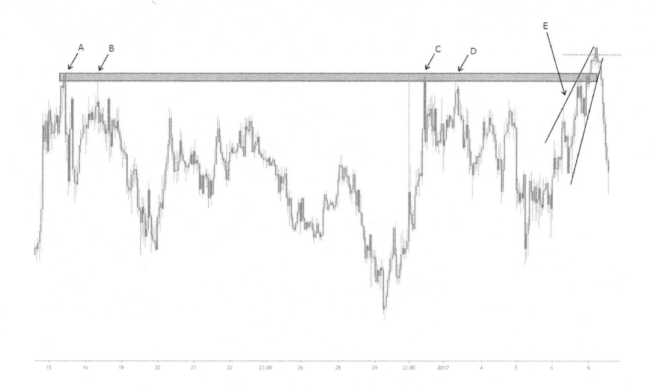

Image 3.1: employing support and resistance, a key component of technical analysis, we can compare TA 1.0 with TA 2.0. The blue zone on the graph, which has numerous rejections (A, B, C, and D), represents a structurally significant resistance level. As soon as the price crosses over the level to the far right of the chart, TA 1.0, which places focus on where the price is, would advise buying. After multiple closes above the level, the green dotted line illustrates where many systems would be buying, signaling that price has successfully overcome any selling resistance the level represented and is now prepared to continue higher. Look instead at E's ascending channel. We can see that although the price did break the resistance level, it did so in the form of a reversal pattern, a corrective ascending structure, which made a drop more likely. The exact point where many technical traders would have entered a long position and suffered a loss using only basic price identification is the exact point where we would have entered a short position and made a profit using the strategies you'll learn later in the book. The chart below explores other variations between TA 1.0 and TA 2.0..

0

A Note on Indicators

The use of numerous technical indicators, in addition to volume bars and moving averages, is another fundamental principle of TA 1.0. No additional signs are necessary for the way I use technical analysis or the method I'll be demonstrating. It's crucial to carefully consider what an indicator actually is and what it stands for. An indicator can only produce indications based on price data that is already shown on the chart. Every indicator, by default, is a lagging market signal that alerts you to an event after it has already happened. Admittedly, different indicators are presenting this data in slightly different ways. The data that they are formed from is information that is already on the chart in the form of the opening, closing, high, and low prices. Some emphasize on momentum, while others look at where price is in reference to an average consensus of value. Of course, I can only speak from personal experience, but it became increasingly clear to me that using indicators did not enhance my trading performance after I carefully studied and applied a number of technical trading indicators, both as standalone tools and as secondary tools to market structure and price action. Instead, the use of these tools distracted me from more significant signals derived from market structure, price patterns, and momentum. Examine the variations in the following charts..

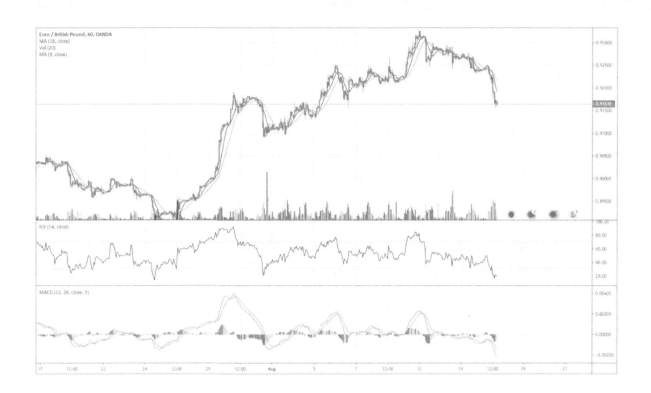

Image 3.2: TA 1.0 trading screen in its typical form. Technical indicators, moving averages, and volume bars are all over the chart. With so much ambiguous and contradictory information available, it can be challenging to comprehend the nature of market movement..

Day Trading? Scalping? Position Trading? Swing Trading?

Depending on the time it takes for a deal to play out and the time period it is done on, many technical trading techniques fit into several categories. A swing trading strategy has deals last between two and five days, whereas a day trading method would have all positions closed before the 24 hour mark. However, a fashion trend could last for weeks or even months. So what about the book's strategy? What place does it have? None of them—and all of them—is the answer. I think TA 1.0 is responsible for this constant urge to lump every system into a strict structure that resembles a box. Instead of rigidly defining trading strategies, we concentrate on taking advantage of the high probability trading opportunities the market presents to us and maximizing our profits. As you'll see, all trades are carried out on either the 1-hour or 15-minute chart, albeit in some cases the position length can range from a few hours to 4 or 5 days. In other words, we let the market take us out regardless of how long it takes by trading in accordance with our precise setups, managing those transactions according to predetermined parameters. The average length of a trade right now is slightly over a day, according to an analysis of my most recent trades. It would be incorrect to assume that I am a day trader in light of this, though. As was previously said, there are numerous instances where positions will last longer..

The Holy Grail to a Deep Understanding of Market Behaviour: Market Structure and Price Action

We'll start our exploration of technical analysis 2.0 after having a clear concept of why it will be our go-to tool for navigating and trading the financial markets. Price movement and market structure come first in that.

Price movement may be thought of as a challenging and difficult concept.

Price action simply refers to price change for the purposes of this work. It's that easy. It depends on what time frame you're looking at and how the market is performing. I'll refer to the market's fluctuations as "price action" because they are dynamic and constantly changing. However, price action is what establishes the market structure. The static records of price history are what are left behind—the observable patterns and structures. We are able to predict the likely direction of prices due to market structure, price movement characteristics, and pattern formation.

Adam Grimes, a well-known trading author, utilized the image of a finger making a pattern in the sand to illustrate the distinction between price action and market structure. Price action is the actual finger movements used to draw the design, whereas market structure is the overall pattern that is left in the sand. The finger may move quickly or slowly, smoothly or erratically, logically or erratically. This is comparable to price activity, which can be swift or gradual, steady or turbulent, logical or chaotic. By maintaining these new values, does the price suggest that following an impulsive upward rise, further continuation is likely, or is the market fast retracing, suggesting that sellers are probably entering at these high prices? Is trading impulsive when the market is moving downward, or is it slowly correcting with low volume and oscillating movement? These traits work together to characterize and define how the market is moving and provide us the short- and long-term directional biases that will enable us to make money from our trades..

Impulses & Corrections

Being able to distinguish between the two stages of market movement—impulses and corrections—is the first step in understanding market structure because it is the later, corrections, that produce observable structures that we will employ in our research. Almost all pricing changes fit into one of these two groups. Price movement can either be corrective or impulsive. You must immediately understand this basic idea because it will serve as the foundation for all that follows. Let's continue exploring each, beginning with impulses, which is possibly the simpler of the two.

Impulses

Sharp price changes with a very obvious directional bias are what define impulses. The market is moving aggressively in the direction it has decided to go. Typically, the flow of institutional money fuels impulses. These market participants have large capital reserves, which when mobilized swiftly, produce powerful directional price movements. They can be quickly identified on the graph and are not arbitrary or interpretable..

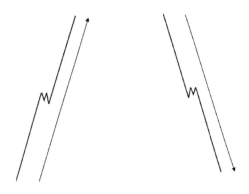

Image 3.4: Examples of impulses

Corrections

Choppy, low volume price swings are a sign of corrective market circumstances. Even though the market is moving, it isn't going with any real conviction. Instead, it is barely moving at all. Corrections can be either rising, descending, or sideways; each of these will be discussed separately in the next paragraphs. What distinguishes an impulse from a correction is not so much the direction it is traveling in as it is the mode of travel. Corrections are once more quite obvious. Asking yourself "Is it an impulse?" is a straightforward technique to determine if something needs to be corrected. Keep in mind that all price changes on the market are either impulsive or corrective. If it's not an impulse, it's automatically a corrective..

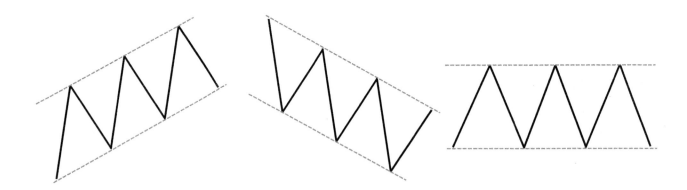

Image 3.5: Examples of corrections

There is much to be said about the accomplishments and discoveries of the market experts who came before me, and that is not what I am bringing to you here. Instead of merely summarizing other trading instructors' ideas, it is my goal to build on their fundamental understanding of market behavior. By doing this, I intend to provide readers a deeper understanding of these concepts and demonstrate how they may be applied to actual trading analysis.

You will discover the precise methods we employ to convert these formations into trading ideas with clear entry and exit locations as well as advice for managing active trades in chapter 7. The strategies you'll learn include CounterPatterns, an advanced set of trades that will extract short-term profits while price is locked in a higher time frame correction, Type 1 entry methods used to capitalize on Bull and Bear Flag continuations, and one that takes advantage of a reversal structure's natural proclivity to breakout as price rejects from the third touch of a reversal channel. Understanding these patterns' directional inclinations, however, is more crucial at this point. Having said that, let's examine each of the five potential outcomes resulting from impulsive and corrective market behavior..

It's as Easy as 1,2,3....4,5

We all know that the market is constantly moving either impulsively or correctively. No matter the market or time frame, all price movement may be divided into one of these two categories. I want to emphasize this idea once again since it is the cornerstone upon which the rest of our discussion will be built. All market movement is either corrective or impulsive, i.e., either it moves quickly with a distinct directional bias or it doesn't; in the latter case, price merely twitches. There can never be a sideways impulse; impulses are always either upwards or downwards by default. However, corrections can be made in one of three directions: up, down, or sideways.

Now that we have this knowledge, we can develop a simplified five-part classification scheme for all potential price fluctuations.:

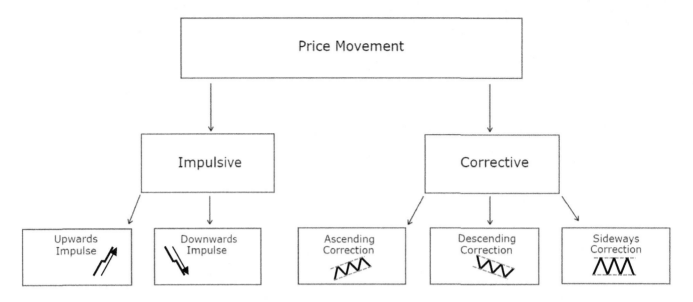

Image 3.6: a condensed representation of all potential price changes. Corrective price movement may move upward, downward, or sideways. Price movements that are impulsive can be upward or downward. As a result, every market movement can be classified into 5 categories of price movement..

Natural Progression

We must comprehend the logical and anticipated price movements that result from each of the movements that make up this system before we can explore each one in detail. I refer to this tendency for the market to proceed in a sequence of logical steps following the establishment of specific pricing structures as "natural progression." The ability to build a directional trading bias based on the present structure is made feasible by being able to identify and categorize the 5 possible price movements.

Let's now examine each of the five price changes, using both the theoretical knowledge of each and the concept of natural development. It is not enough to simply acknowledge the existence of any of these patterns; every market observation must be supported by a sound theoretical foundation. What I'm saying is that it's important to be able to explain why certain price patterns exist in the market rather than just observing and acknowledging their presence. Having a better understanding of why something happens rather than just observing it makes us more confident in our trade.

The two simplest yet most fundamental patterns that characterize market movements are upward and downward impulses. These strong price changes occur across all markets and time frames and are the basis of our study..

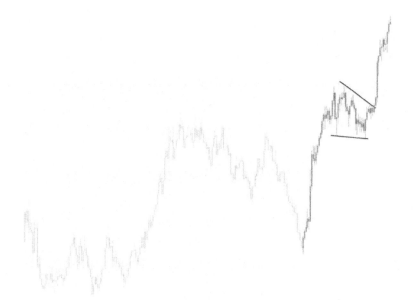

Euro / Japanese Yen, 1D, OANDA

Image 3.7: Two distinct upward directed impulses separated by a brief corrective. The market has risen sharply in comparison to all prior price movement, making the impulses simple to identify. The market is moving upward due to intense purchasing demand..

Natural progression

Usually, significant institutional interest is what drives impulses. Deep, liquid markets don't act rashly without the support of sizable capital reserves. A small corrective pattern followed by another upward impulsive advance is the logical evolution after an upward impulsive surge. Take into account the normal procedure used by huge organizations to build up a sizable stake. These institutions typically buy in batches. They will only purchase a portion of their desired position in order to avoid flooding the market with demand. The market starts to consolidate as the initial buying urges fade. The market is currently caught in a range that will either be sideways or contrary to the previous impulse due to an equilibrium of purchasing and selling pressure. There are many names we can give price action of this kind, including pullbacks, corrections, and consolidations, but regardless of the precise name we give it, they are all functionally equivalent in that they all describe what is happening: a pause, consolidating the energy of the previous impulse, probably in anticipation of another impulse in the same direction. Consider carefully what the correction is accusing. The market has made an impulsive upward move, and the price is holding at these current levels. Since there has not been any selling pressure, it is likely that interest and buying pressure are still high. The institutions continue their buying activity after it had stalled during the low momentum correction, and as a result of individual retail traders joining in for the ride up, the supply and demand equation flips to the contrary side. Price breaks out of the consolidation zone as a result of the appearance of this second surge of momentum, indicating the likelihood of another impulsive move. This is the progression of the market naturally: the initial upswing (1), a sideways or downward corrective channel (2), and then another upswing impulsively (3). This straightforward three-part impulse, correction, impulse pattern occurs statistically so frequently that it serves as the foundation for two of the setups you will learn about in chapter 7, Bull and Bear Flags.

This straightforward yet profound pattern is most remarkable since it consistently repeats itself over any period of time. Finding examples of the same impulse-correction-impulse pattern is simple, whether you are looking at a trend that has lasted years across two currencies or a trend that only lasts a few hours within a single day. I frequently make fun of other traders about how frequently this pattern appears because, once you train your eye to recognize them, the proverb "once you see it, you can't un-see it" actually rings true. Once you have gotten used to recognizing this pattern, you won't be able to ignore the numerous times it appears. Examine picture 3.8 below..

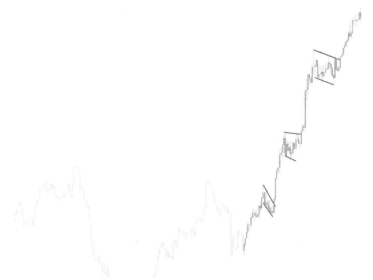

Image 3.8: There have been numerous instances of upward impulses followed by sideways or downward corrective patterns. This is just how markets develop naturally. It is understandable why we would be anticipating greater price continuation following an upward impulsive movement and a correction..

Think about a different scenario. The market increases rashly. Instead of the market correcting, traders who believe these newer, higher prices are simply too high become anxious to engage short, pushing the supply and demand equation to the supply side. The next outcome is a swift retracement of the prior impulse, as seen in figure 3.9. This is not an organic development..

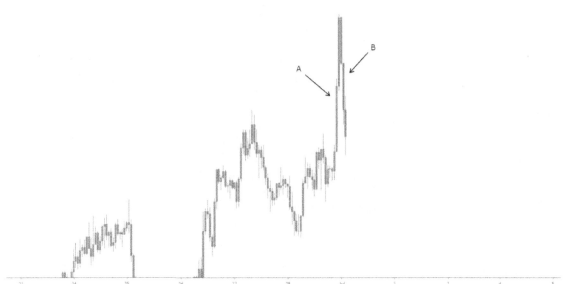

Image 3.9: The market experiences a significant upward movement (A). Price quickly retraces (B), as opposed to correcting sideways, which would indicate additional continuation is likely. This is not an organic development..

Impulsively Downwards

Image 3.10: Two distinct downward directed impulses separated by a brief corrective. The market has fallen down sharply in comparison to all preceding price activity, making the impulses simple to identify. Strong selling pressure is pushing the market downward..

Natural progression

As we've just seen, the price making impulsive, momentum-driven swings out of periods of contracted volatility is one of the most common and quantifiable features of technical analysis. The downward impulse is completely consistent with the notion that we just described for the upward impulse. But first, a quick recap of the mechanisms.

Market fall has been pushed by intense selling pressure. In light of recent trade and price movement, the move appears impulsive. Most likely, a significant round of institutional selling activity was what sparked the sell-off. However, and this is a crucial lesson, you shouldn't worry about the precise reason for the sell-off. Avoid attempting to comprehend every market activity. You'll only fill your head with unimportant things if you do this. Simply acknowledge that movement is occurring and take advantage of it by identifying precise entry points that are consistent with your plan.

However, there has been a significant downward movement in the market. According to natural progression, the first step is to observe a corrective pattern that either moves laterally or in the opposite direction (ascending) of the initial impulse. Another downward impulse results from a successful breakout as the selling pressure keeps building. The three-part pattern is the same as before—impulse, correction, impulse—it has only been inverted to the downward. Please see the picture below..

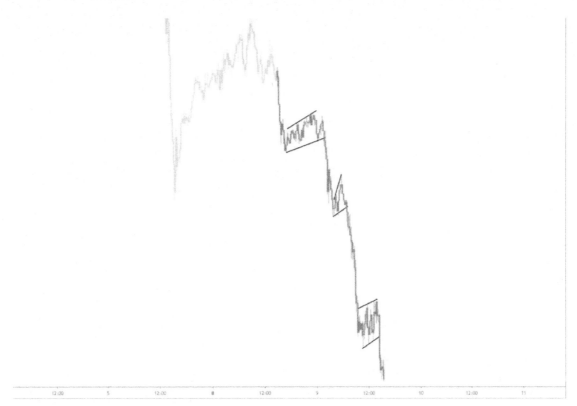

Image 3.11: numerous instances of downward impulses followed by patterns of ascending or sideways consolidation. This is just how markets develop naturally. It is clear why we would favor further price continuance after witnessing a negative impulsive movement and a pullback..

The other potential scenario is that the market experiences immediate purchasing pressure after an impulse to the downside rather than correcting in expectation of another move lower. These decreased prices have been assessed by traders to be sufficiently low to justify a purchase position. They see this as an opportunity to get goods at a great area of value because of the low pricing. If many traders and operators share this opinion, a swift retrace of the prior impulse, as seen in image 3.12, is the expected outcome. This is not an organic development..

Image 3.12: A powerful downward impulse (A) is promptly followed by a similarly strong upward motion that completely retraces the impulse's path. This is not a normal market development.
A sideways or opposite-to-the-preceding-impulse adjustment is required before a downward descent like A can continue. This shows that the market is able to maintain its newly high price levels and is prepared to resume its impulsive trajectory after the correction has been successfully broken..

Now let's talk about corrections. Corrections are choppy price movements in which the price is simply circling in either an upward, downward, or sideways direction. Because of the different forms that corrections might take, they are fundamentally more complicated than impulses. Contrary to impulses, corrections can be visualized as distinct price patterns on the chart, such as ascending or descending channels. Because there are so many different formations that could occur, these structures are more complicated than impulses. Although there may be very slight variations in length and shape, as well as directional bias, the natural development of these channels is very straightforward: they are reversal structures. A structure known as a reversal pattern indicates that price is more likely to go against the direction of the channel. We can anticipate the next urge and put ourselves in the right place by developing our ability to recognize these structures. If this concept initially seems unclear, do not be disheartened; we will discuss numerous examples of this concept in this chapter and in chapter 7 on trading setups..

Correctively Upwards

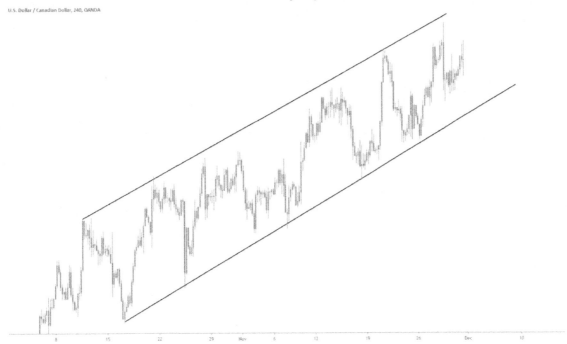

Image 3.13: Price is rising in a corrective manner and has formed a broad ascending channel.
At least three distinct rejection points on either the top or bottom of the pattern are a defining feature of ascending channels. These channels often signal the possibility of a negative trend reversal..

Natural Progression

An upward or upward correction signals that the market is running out of steam and that its current trajectory cannot be sustained without a prior decline to the downside. Consider what the channel's presence indicates: the market is losing momentum; there isn't enough underlying buying pressure to push the market up impulsively; instead, the price can only gently drip upward. There is little intrinsic buying power in such a move, and when the slight buying pressure eventually wanes, the outcome is frequently an abrupt downward move as the price breaks through the channel..

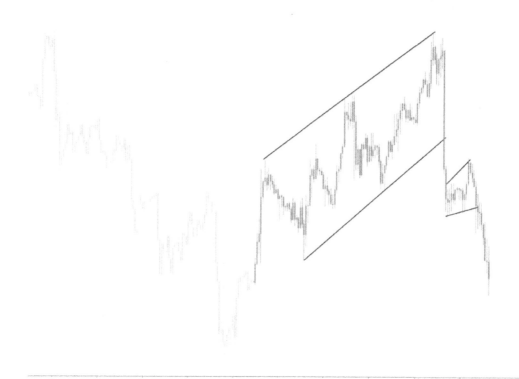

Image 3.14: Price abruptly breaks to the negative after building an upward corrective channel. This evolution is inevitable. Examine how price broke the channel on the right side of the chart using the impulse, correction, impulse pattern that we just looked at..

Now think about the alternate scenario: the creation of an ascending channel, and instead of a breakout to the downside, price pushes to the upward, escaping the confines of its current structure. Even though these patterns' statistical tendencies indicate that this is the less likely possibility, it is still a possibility. These patterns do not have 100% reliability, nor are they entirely impregnable. However, they do, more often than not, give us important hints about the market's likely course. The pattern just didn't play out when it wasn't supposed to, as natural evolution would suggest. Below, I've given a specific illustration of such a circumstance..

Image 3.15: In opposition to the directional forecast the ascending channel offered, the price impulsively breaks out to the upside. This is not an organic development..

Correctively Downwards

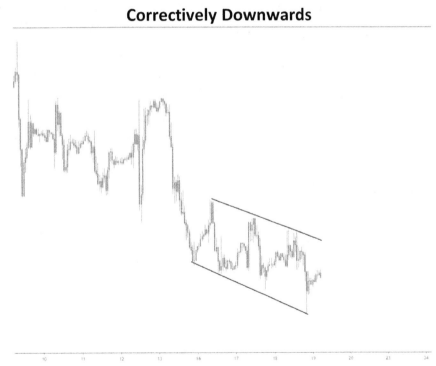

Image 3.16: Price moving correctively to the downside, forming a descending channel.

Descending channels are characterized by at least 3 clear rejection points on either the top or bottom of the pattern. These channels typically indicate a potential reversal to the upside is in play.

Natural Progression

The ascending adjustment we discussed in the previous section may be applied to the descending channel using the same theory and guidelines: Descending corrections that form reversal channels frequently cause price to move in the opposite direction of its current orientation. A downward correction signals that the market's momentum is wearing off and that the current direction of the market's movement is unsustainable.

The market is losing momentum, as indicated by a descending channel, and is only able to slowly drip price downward because there isn't enough underlying selling pressure to propel the market down impulsively. There is no intrinsic selling force in this movement, and when the slight selling pressure eventually fades, the price frequently moves impulsively upward and out of the channel..

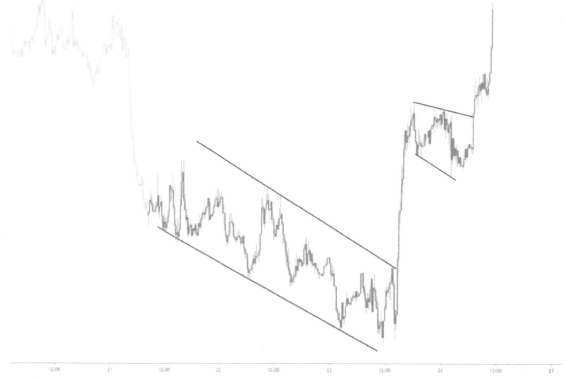

Image 3.17: Price impulsively breaks to the upside after creating a falling corrective channel. This evolution is inevitable. Examine how the price

breached the channel on the right side of the chart using the impulse, correction, impulse pattern that we just looked at.

The alternative situation, of course, is a pattern failure, in which the price simply keeps falling abruptly, as shown in the chart below..

Image 3.18:: A declining channel develops, but instead of confirming the channel's directional bias, the price declines to the negative. This is not an organic development..

Correctively Sideways

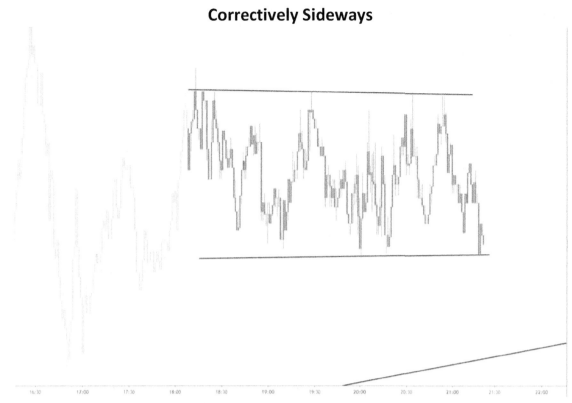

Image 3.19: Price moving correctively sideways.

Natural Progression

The third and final iteration of the adjustment has a somewhat different set of rules than its ascending and descending siblings. If the previous move was an impulse, these sideways structures often act as a continuation pattern. Extended sideways corrections are essentially random price action with no usefulness for our trading. They take place in the unpredictability of price movement and are not preceded by any apparent directional impulses. An example of one such channel is shown in image 3.19 above. While sideways, it is just random back and forth movement without any discernible impulse. However, if the preceding movement had been a significant upward impulse followed by the development of a sideways channel, logic would dictate that more upward movement is likely. The channel is currently serving as a pause and consolidating before the upcoming surge of momentum. Review the minor adjustments to the up and down impulses that we saw in the first two parts. These minor patterns emerged after the initial impulses. Larger, but otherwise quite similar, are sideways adjustments.

These 5 types of price movement offer a great starting point for evaluating and analyzing price movement. Although the aforementioned examples are a purposefully oversimplified way of viewing the markets, they do offer the

46

trader a straightforward and uniform labeling regime. This framework will be crucial when we examine the specific 5 trade examples in chapter 7.

As we will see in Multiple Time Frame Analysis, when we examine the complexity of what I refer to as the Matrix of the Market, market movements are intrinsically complicated and can occasionally fit into more than one of these movements. However, it suffices to just comprehend the fundamentals of these 5 actions and the predicted natural advancement of each at this point in your development. I advise you to carefully review this foundation before moving on. Start by identifying these different types of market movement on the charts of some of your favorite stocks or currency pairs during the time frame of your choice. Look for instances of impulsive and corrective market behavior. Using the tools provided by your charting supplier, sketch in the corrections roughly. You will benefit immensely from your trade when you develop the ability to distinguish between these two periods as we continue to develop and broaden your technical toolbox.

The Beginning of the Correction: Key Inflection Points

Ascending and descending corrections frequently result in price reversals, as we learned in the preceding section. We cannot, however, assume that extended trends will follow every successful breakout. Of course, if you have previously entered a trade on or before the breakout, this is the ideal result. However, being aware of the anticipated termination points will help you manage your expectations for the trade. The first defined touch point of the correction is one of the first likely termination points for the fresh impulse. This turning point must to be taken into account as a potential profit objective or at the very least serve as the initial location where traders ought to be on the lookout for indications of potential failure.

The two charts below illustrate.

Image 3.20: When the channel successfully breaks out, the beginning of the correction could serve as an inflection point. As you can see in this illustration, price hits level A after the channel has broken before staging a big negative reversal. Use the ray line tool in TradingView to create a horizontal line starting at the beginning of the correction..

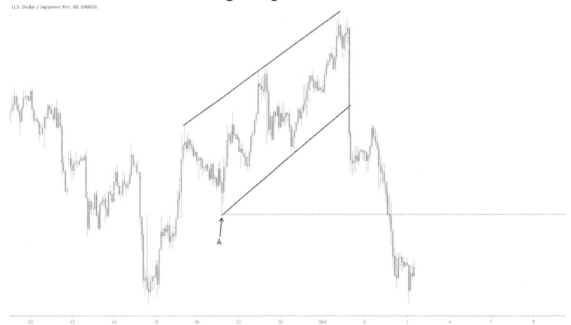

Image 3.21: An additional channel bending possibility in an ascending one. This illustration demonstrates how these areas are simply potential areas of interest and are not always regions of reversal. Price moved across the level in this instance as if it didn't even exist..

Drawing Structure

I'm hoping that at this time you've started to apply some of the knowledge you've learned so far to your personal situation after internalizing some of the information presented so far. These epiphanies are known as "uh-huh" moments. That's great. That proves that you are aware of the real-world applications of what I've just spoken and how they might help your trading. You now realize that the market is divided into two separate phases: impulsive price swings and corrective price movements. As you are aware, corrections frequently result in unique price structures that we can recognize and depict on the chart. The actual identifying and drawing of these structures is the next logical and natural step in your instruction.

We all know that people, or the entities buying and selling in the markets, are what cause price changes. We may translate this human psychology into graphical, visual representations that help us swiftly evaluate the state of the market and the likely probable and conceivable scenarios for price movement by drawing in structure and pricing patterns. Therefore, one of the most crucial technical skills you'll learn as a trader is how to accurately identify and depict relevant market structure.

We'll take a "top down" approach to drawing structure, gradually zooming in on the market action to gain a comprehensive grasp of how price is changing. Starting with the daily and 4-hour charts, we'll work our way down to the 1-hour chart, occasionally using the 15-minute chart for more precision and fine-tuning.

It's necessary to have procedures and an established process in place because determining the appropriate market structure might become subjective. Key is consistency. There are only 4 easy steps.

Step 1 Determine Support and Resistance

Determine the pertinent support and resistance zones starting with the daily chart. These ought to be visibly distinct reversal zones. Look for price levels where the trend has changed at least twice, ideally three times.

One of the most basic yet basic elements of technical analysis are these levels. Support levels can be conceptualized as a price level where there is sufficient demand to halt or even reverse a price decrease. For resistance levels, the definition is the opposite. Imagine support and resistance levels as floors and ceilings, respectively, that could be able to stop price from rising/falling any further. This may make understanding them easier. The idea that markets have memories is one of the fundamentals of technical analysis. Important price levels where the price has previously reversed can serve as important turning points in the future. It is simple to understand why this is the case: traders will logically be keeping an eye on levels where price has reversed two or more times, possibly even using such levels as the basis for their buy or sell decisions. Think of a market that is declining. A support level that has previously served as the catalyst for several price reversals is getting near as price continues to fall to the downside. Traders that are short begin selling their holdings as price approaches, believing that additional downward movement is unlikely. The same goes for traders who are patiently waiting with their buy orders, ready to go long as soon as the price reaches the critical level and anticipate the bullish reversal. The selling pressure will be sufficiently offset by the pent-up liquidity at these levels to halt or even reverse the price slide. You may once more use the inverse relationship to describe a resistance level in a bull market. Because the theoretical idea is so plain, many traders are tempted to overemphasize it. It is simple for new traders to believe that buying at support and selling at resistance is all there is to trading. However, because there are so many fundamental and technical factors at play in the markets, it is simple to identify numerous potential instances of support and resistance levels, the majority of which are identical to one another. Therefore, we must limit our attention to the zones found on the higher time scales that are the most structurally significant..

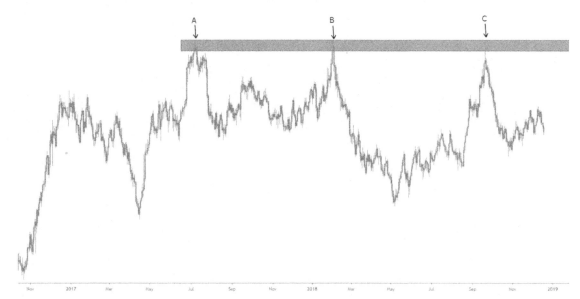

Image 3.22: On the daily chart, drawing structure is started by locating the most likely support and resistance areas. Mark the zone on your chart using TradingView's rectangle tool for future reference. The defined rejections off the level at A, B, and C are shown here. After the first two hits (A & B), traders may have recognized this area as a probable zone of reversal, which was confirmed when the price rejected for the third time at C. One last word on C. B is rejected in late April 2018, whilst C was rejected in the beginning of September 2018. Even after waiting over six months, the level was still fundamentally important. Markets are not forgetful.

Step 2: Define the Current Structure

Find the most recent impulsive leg on the daily chart, linking the important highs and lows that came after. You should be able to begin defining and drawing the existing structure as long as you can connect 2 distinct rejections on both the highs and lows. Keep in mind that the structure we're trying to find appears following the most recent market impulse. From this longer time horizon perspective, if it appears to be impulsive and there are no obvious patterns, just move on to the next phase..

Image 3.23: Find the most recent leg of a clear impulse (A) on the daily and then connect the important highs and lows of the structure that followed (red circles)..

Step 3: Refine on the 4-hour

Use the 4-hour chart for extra precision.

Image 3.24: Refine the trendlines you have discovered from the daily chart on the 4-hour chart. Connect them to the arrows' wicks..

Step 4: Drill Down to the 1-hour

Locate and mark any structure on the 1-hour chart that isn't obvious on the higher time frames as you drill down to it..

Image 3.25: Draw the structures that are concealed on the longer time periods using the 1-hour chart. The same guidelines apply as before: locate the most recent impulse move (A) and join the highs and lows of the subsequent pattern (red circles)..

Probable Vs Possible

The dynamic realities of price movements make it typical to notice numerous potential price patterns and possibilities at once when you start to detect and draw in structure. This is what I mean by "likely and possible." Because different structures might indicate distinct directional biases and contradicting signals, this can be perplexing for new traders. This need not be a negative for us, either. In fact, as the illustration below shows, keeping track of a variety of potential forms and structures can help us manage trades, find potential reversal points, and identify alternate trade entrances in the event that our preferred forecast is incorrect..

Image 3.26: the likely and conceivable. There were several price structures found, each with a distinct directional prediction. I can recognize the higher-probability structures (the probable) in solid lines while still being aware of the alternative situations (the possible) in dotted lines by employing two different types of lines. A distinct correction channel is present in this instance (solid lines). After a significant impulse, price then creates a distinct Bull Flag (A). I go long on the break of A because I anticipate a big channel break and a probable move to the beginning of the correction (blue line). Another corrective pattern appears to be forming as the price moves forward (B). I use dotted lines to depict the new channel in order to represent the other potential outcome because it is still likely that we will continue to experience upward.

A second, more narrow channel (C), within the broader B channel, forms as a result of continued price development.

Given the other two options, I understand it is likely that a price reversal will occur near the intersection of the two potential channels (red circle). If price shows symptoms of reversal at that time, I can exit the original long position profitably and start to shift my bias and hunt for short entry points. I continue to be neural because I am aware that there are various possibilities for price movement and that I do not need to be bound by a single, inflexible expectation in order to be profitable. This is a fundamental quality of profitable traders..

Invalidated Structures

Every building we locate comes with a unique directional forecast. A correction that is climbing has a negative bias, one that is descending has a bullish bias, etc. But of course, nothing in trading works 100 percent of the time. These systems are not faultless. Occasionally, they are mistaken. The rational and likely directed forecast doesn't always come true. So how do we determine whether a structure is still viable and if not, why not? How do we tell when that pattern's trading utility is no longer present?

Three crucial events—a break of the pattern against its directional bias, a continuation pattern, and a second impulsive move away—signal that a pattern has been invalidated. Before examining a genuine market case, let's go through each in more detail.

Step One: The initial impulsive breakout of the structure in the direction opposite the directional bias the pattern supplies is the first requirement. Consider a corrective channel that ascends. Probability indicates that this will eventually break down to the downside. Your first indication that something has changed is if price moves out of the channel abruptly, forcefully, and to the upside. The price has entered the channel in the opposite direction of what we predicted.

Step two: Following the first impulse out, there is a continuance. A single impulse from a structure is insufficient. Before declaring there has been a true breach, we must observe a correction. Consider the market in terms of natural progression at all times. Always consider "what happens next?" if pricing abruptly departs from the established structure or trend. Is it correcting, in which case the move will likely continue, or is price already retracing into the initial pattern?

Step three: Following the correction, there is a continuation. Price's recent impulsive movement away from the correction is proof that the original move that disrupted the structure has been sufficiently followed up on..

Image 3.27: Price is moving inside of an ascending channel, which portends a breakout to the negative.

However, in opposition to this directional bias, price impulsively bursts out of the channel (A) by moving upward (step one). After that, price makes a tight correction (B), indicating that there may be underlying purchasing demand supporting a move higher (step 2). In the final step (step three), price resumes its initial movement (C) in the form of another impetus. The first rising channel is no longer viable because all three requirements have been satisfied. Price lost any useful trading benefit or directional forecast the instant it broke out at C.

There is proof that a structure has lost its validity when all three of these circumstances have taken place. These first two criteria by themselves are sufficient proof that a structure invalidation is likely. Natural progression, however, demands us to wait until all 3 phases have been completed before declaring a structure to be flawed. There is no advancement if, after the initial impulse out of the structure, price travels back into the pattern rather than completing stages 2 and 3. It can be creating a brand-new structure or a bigger one. The next stage is to review the structure and perhaps make changes to it..

When There's No Progression, Evolve

Structure is not a set, permanent item of furniture for the market. Market structures are probably going to change as price action takes shape. Larger variations of patterns or even completely new price patterns might form as they expand. What initially appears to be a narrow ascending channel may eventually enlarge to become a much wider channel. <u>As crucial as first seeing structure is knowing when to evolve it</u>. So, how do we determine when to change a pattern and when it should just be invalidated?

Keep in mind that we always consider the market in terms of natural development. Let's quickly recap the definition of natural progression: it is the markets' natural movement; it is their propensity to move in a succession of impulses and corrections. The market goes impulsively in one way, makes a correction, and then resumes its movement as another impulse. With this perspective on the market, it stands to reason that a correction would follow an impulsive break before another impulse away as a result of natural progression. It is the straightforward three-step procedure that we discussed in the previous section. What about a different scenario, though? What if following the breakout, price just retraces back into the original structure as seen in the graphic below, rather than witnessing a correction and another impulse away (steps 2 and 3)? Simply by changing the channel, we can now incorporate this new price movement..

Image 3.28: the identical channel as in picture 3.27. Price moves in the opposite direction of the directional bias (A). Price then returns right away to the original structure. Since steps two and three have not been met, there has been no natural advancement. We may now adapt the structure to reflect the most recent price movement, as shown below..

Image 3.29: It has evolved the channel. The solid line depicts the developed shape including the new price action, whereas the dotted line depicts the original structure. In terms of structure, nothing has changed despite the abrupt breakout; this is still an ascending reversal channel with a downside tilt. The aforementioned chart examples show when and how to move forward when the price breaks out in the opposite direction of the correction's directional projection. How and when then, do we evolve when price breaks out in the anticipated direction? Applying the idea of natural evolution, the same guidelines apply. Study the following examples carefully.

The market has been correctively moving into a crucial area of resistance. Price has been trickling inside of two convergent trendlines as the correction has created an upward channel. Price abruptly breaks the channel as it approaches the resistance level. A tidy tiny corrective pattern is then formed as price corrects. The market has impulsively broken the reversal channel, the correction has indicated that there is enough selling pressure at these lower levels to prevent a retracement to the upside, and another downward move is now likely. This is a natural progression. Natural progression has confirmed that the adjustment has occurred as expected..

Image 3.30: As it approaches a crucial level of higher time frame resistance (not indicated), price has been trading in a corrective manner, producing an ascending channel. At A, the price abruptly departs from the channel. Price then develops a corrective (B), indicating that further decline is likely. At C, the price is continuing to rise. This evolution is inevitable.

Let's now examine the identical situation with a different possibility, one in which natural growth is not possible. As before, an ascending channel is heading toward a significant area of resistance. We are biased to the downside by default. In order to validate our bias and to wait for the first continuation pattern for a trade, we watch for price to successfully breach the reversal channel. Price does, in fact, abruptly breach the channel, but instead of developing a continuation pattern, it instantly returns to the first channel. Price was unable to maintain the new low pricing; instead, it encountered persistent buying pressure, which forced it back into the original structure. This is not a natural development. While the price did breach the channel in the form of an impulse, it was clear that there wasn't enough selling pressure to sustain this move because there was no little corrective. In other words, there wasn't any advancement. We can modify the structure to take into account this new price action because price returned to the original channel. Although the pattern may have changed a little, the structure still supports our original hypothesis that this is a reversal channel headed downward. It's crucial to avoid "marrying" our trendlines and patterns. They are arbitrary tools with only one objective: to assist us in determining the status of the market as it is at that particular moment..

Image 3.31: same television channel as before. Price, however, soon retraced back into the old pattern after breaking out at A. Consequently, there hasn't been any market growth..

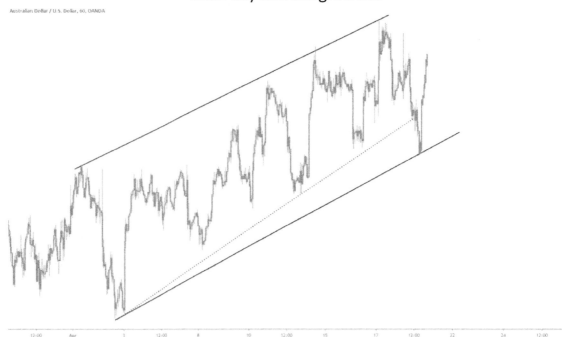

Image 3.32: In order to accommodate the new price action, the structure has altered. The solid lines depict the pattern's evolution into a more parallel price channel while the dotted lines depict the pattern's original structure. The original pattern is still a corrective ascending channel with a downside reversal tendency, and its structural integrity has not changed. However, recent price movement has altered its precise structure and configuration..

Drawing Structure: An Assignment

Your market structure master lesson is now complete. Now that you have the necessary resources, you can begin finding pertinent structures. You also have the rules necessary to determine when a structure is no longer viable and when it needs to be updated to reflect new price action.

I would want to encourage you to spend some time applying the information you have learned to your own charts with an assignment of sorts before we go onto the last piece of the puzzle that will give us a comprehensive grasp of market structure and price movement. Use the framework and guidelines from the preceding sections to start spotting structures on the charts of your favorite stocks or currency pairs. As the structure is broken, watch how the price moves. Use the 3-step method to identify situations where you would have invalidated a structure that didn't behave as you had anticipated and those where you would have changed the structure to reflect new price action. You can use TradingView's bar replay tool to rewind price activity and prevent future price action from appearing in your screen. I advise carrying out this activity on the 4-hour chart with the goal of going through a year's worth of price data across a few different assets. This practice will expand your comprehension of the nature of these structures on a more subconscious level while also assisting in the improvement of your pattern detection abilities. You will be able to witness for yourself the extreme regularity with which these structures operate and the ensuing price movement. Once you are completely comfortable with the material we have covered so far, move on to the following section where we start to investigate the complexities of numerous time frames.

Analysis over Multiple Time Frames: The Market's Matrix

Financial markets are fractal by nature, which means that the structures and patterns that are produced on the daily chart are also built on smaller time frames. Patterns are produced by the combination of price activity on the 5-minute chart and the 15-minute chart, the hourly chart and the 4-hour chart, and so on. The end result is an infinite variety of interwoven patterns from various time frames, all of which hint and indicate various potential price changes. This is what I refer to as the market matrix. The trader must comprehend this idea because it is crucial. No pattern exists in a vacuum; the pattern that is being seen on one time frame is composed of structures that are comparable on a lower time frame. One of the biggest performance-enhancing principles a trader might learn is to comprehend this idea. Applying it to your trading could help you avoid many aggravating, frequently avoidable losses and improve your ability to profit from your winning deals. The concept that time frames are not one dimensional and operate alone must be accepted by traders. Instead, they are bound together irrevocably. This is why our work in this section, which focuses on various time frame analysis, is so crucial.

Without it, market analysis would be unable to achieve the same level of depth and comprehension that multiple time frame (MTF) analysis brings. My response would be straightforward if I had to sum up the importance of many time frame analyses in a single word: context. Structures are placed on one time frame in the context of higher time frames via MTF analysis. Trading professionals can more accurately determine their entry points, screen out trades, and handle their trades more effectively by using MTF analysis. Our major entry time frames are the 1-hour and 15-minute charts, however their sole function is to find high probability entry and exit locations. But the higher time periods are what form the foundation of the overall analysis and directional bias. In other words, the higher time frames serve as the foundation for every deal we make.

The daily and four-hour charts are the longer time spans for our purposes. They assist in giving us a larger perspective by illuminating the dominating trend. We use the shorter time frames—the 1-hour and 15-minute charts—to pinpoint exact trade entry points. Consider them like obtaining binoculars and using them to examine the 4-hour and daily charts' individual candles with greater detail.

Due to two factors, learning this body of knowledge may be challenging. The first is that beginning traders almost never tackle the material until properly comprehending the structures and their ramifications on a single time frame. This creates one significant issue: until you are proficient in reading a chart in a single time frame, it is impossible to understand the nuances of many time frames. MTF analysis can be challenging for novice traders for a second reason: it cannot be easily reduced to a straightforward rule set or procedure. This section seeks to investigate these common denominators and recurring ideas as well as their actual trading consequences.

Beginning with the upper time frames and moving downward, we'll begin our study of the time frames by using a top-down approach. We'll show concrete examples of how MTF analysis may help us make better trading selections..

Higher Time Frames

The daily and 4-hour charts have higher time frames. They are typically more important than the shorter time intervals. Practically speaking, higher time frame knowledge can eliminate lower time frame trades and increase trade confidence by identifying the market's current state, whether it is corrective or impulsive, and enabling us to predict the likely directional momentum. Let's examine each one in turn, along with concrete suggestions for improving your own real-world trading analysis.

Choosing Trades

The first application is as a filter for trades on lower time frames that are out of sync with the directional bias on higher time frames. An important illustration of what would have been regarded as a promising setup for a short position on the 1-hour chart is shown in Image 3.35. The strong falling impulse was followed by a corrective that points to the potential for a breakout beneath the flag..

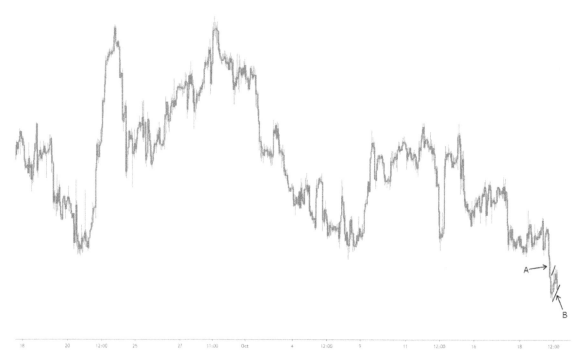

Image 3.33: Many traders may be searching for a setup to get short this pair because they believe that the strong negative impulse at A and the corrective price action at B will lead to more downward pressure..

Does this seem like a solid short setup from this angle? You would have been 100% correct if you had said, "I am not sure, I need more context and information." Although the conditions for a short have been met from this time frame, **a trader must first comprehend what is happening from a wider perspective in order to draw any reliable trading conclusions**.

This flag was contained in what was more likely a Bull Flag, a slightly downward corrective with an upside bias, according to the higher time frame (the daily chart), which supplied important context..

Image 3.34: The daily chart of the same pair at the same time as the chart above clearly contradicts the hourly chart's bearish tenor. From this angle, we can observe that the price actually built a smaller continuation structure at C after breaking out of the descending channel (A) in the form of an impulse (B). It is likely that this move will continue, at least to the beginning of the correction (blue line), according to natural market progression. Knowing that the longer-term directional forecast was bullish, you could have ignored the short setup on the previous chart in favor of looking for setups that aligned with the structure and momentum of the higher time frames. If you had chosen to go short in the first chart without understanding the context that the higher time frame perspective was providing, you would have lost money as the higher time frame Bull Flag took over and drove price to the upside..

A wonderful illustration of temporal frames providing contradicting directional messages is this one. In this case, the higher time frame exhibits a bullish leaning and displays a Bull Flag that contrasts with the hourly time frame's smaller Bear Flag pattern. Of course, the daily Bull Flag can end up failing and aggressively breaking out to the downside, but in this case, the odds are in favor of a price move upward. Additionally, as traders, we always seek to align ourselves with what the probability indicate.

Always give preference to the directional bias presented by the higher time frame over the directional bias shown by the lower time frame.

It's important to repeat and underline the previous clause because it could prevent you from suffering a lot of heartbreaking losses. Look to position yourself in the same direction on the lower time frames once the directional bias on the higher time frames has been established. Always be mindful of patterns on lower time frames that conflict with patterns on higher time frames, at the very least. You will discover an advanced trading method in chapter 7 that enables you to use the CounterPattern setup to trade against the higher time frame directional forecast.

Identifying Current Market Structure/Phase

Determining whether the HTF is presently in an impulsive or corrective stage is the technical trader's most crucial task. In order to locate entry points on the lower time frame in the same direction (discussed shortly), it is helpful to understand the phase we are in. If the HTF is in the impulsive phase, we can locate straightforward continuation trades using the lower time frames. We can use the lower time frames to trade inside the boundaries of the structure if the HTF is in a corrective situation. Below, each is covered.

Impulsive at a Higher Time Frame

Traders thrive in these circumstances. These conditions can create a number of continuation trades at lower time frames that feed into the momentum of the HTF when it is experiencing considerable directional price movement. Keep in mind that events occurring in one time frame are composed of smaller structures occurring in earlier time frames. Lower time frame impulses and corrections are most likely what make up an impulsive condition on the HTF. While momentum is active on the HTF, we can uncover straightforward setups that resolve in the same direction by keeping an eye on price action on these lower time frames..

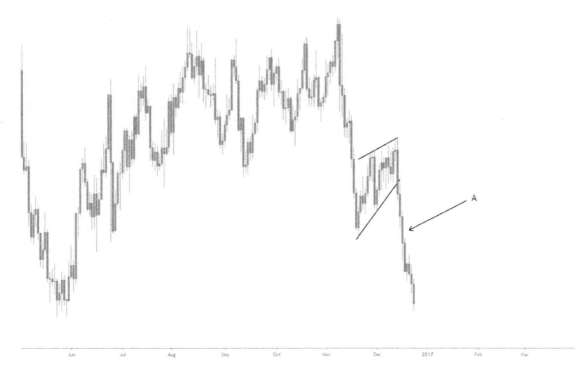

Image 3.35: The AUD/USD daily chart. Point A has a single, unambiguous directional impulse. Lower time frames might offer straightforward setups in these circumstances when the HTF is moving impulsively, as shown in the chart below..

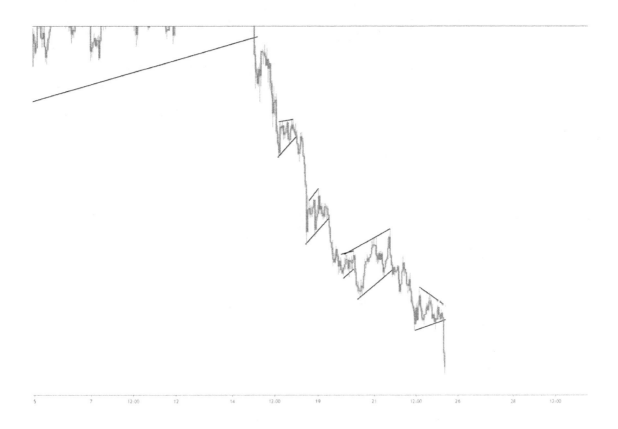

Image 3.36: the same pair's hourly time period. The HTF impulsive leg is actually composed of a number of smaller, lower time frame impulses and corrections, giving traders a number of opportunities to profit from the move. Depending on the management techniques employed, each of the structures mentioned below would have produced a transaction that was either lucrative or breakeven. Chapter 7 will teach you how to take advantage of situations like this..

Higher Time Frame Is Corrective

The idea that the market has two distinct phases—impulsive and corrective—is probably familiar to you if you've read this far. However, there is another crucial point that may be a little trickier to grasp: there may be lower time frame impulsive legs within a higher time frame correction. The paradox is that what appears to be a highly corrective structure on the higher time frame might, on the lower time frame, be composed of a number of tradeable impulses. Don't worry if something at first looks unclear. Soon, we'll talk about some sample charts. Just keep in mind that even if price is currently trapped in an HTF correction, we can trade and benefit from the market while we wait for the more lucrative impulsive conditions.

The daily chart is displayed in Image 3.37. The market has started to consolidate and form a correction after a sharp explosive upward rise. Many traders could write off a market that is constrained in this way, preferring to get involved once the correction successfully breaks, anticipating the start of the impulsive phase. However, inside longer time period corrective structures, some of the simplest and cleanest trades take place. Think carefully about the examples that follow because this is a crucial but frequently misunderstood component of market analysis..

Image 3.37: The daily chart shows the market is locked in a slightly ascending/sideways corrective structure. Many traders prefer to dismiss markets in these corrective conditions, preferring to wait for a break and for the market to start its impulsive phase.

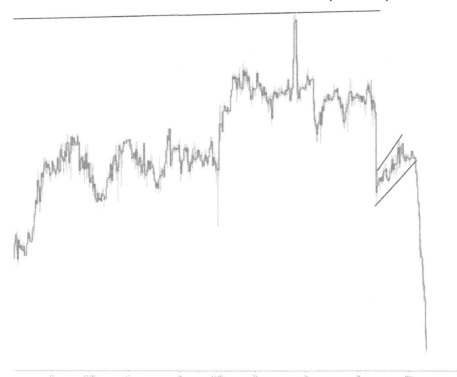

Image 3.38: Despite being contained within the upper time frame correction, the lower time frame offers a high-probability trading opportunity to the downside. Of course, this is a clean example that was chosen on purpose, but the idea is still valid: high-quality trades can develop within HTF corrective

structures, especially with regards to straightforward flag patterns like these (discussed in chapter 7)..

Lower Time Frames

Keep in mind the four-time frame structure, which consists of two higher and two lower time frames. The 15-minute and 1-hour charts are shown here. As you are aware, the longer time horizons offer priceless data in the form of a broader context. The lower time frames, in contrast, are only utilized to precisely clock entry into the higher time frame patterns and structures. Despite the fact that I have mentioned two lower time frames, the 1-hour chart is the one that is most frequently utilized, with the 15-minute chart just serving to further refine what is seen on the 1-hour. We'll go over each of the individual tasks of the shorter time frames, beginning with the 1-hour chart, to clear up any misunderstandings.

The 1-hour Chart: Timing Entries

The lower time frames are simply instruments for locating entry points into price movements on the more structurally significant HTFs, as I have already indicated on numerous occasions. Consider the scenario when your research identified a corrective continuation pattern on the daily chart. You've created a positive price bias by anticipating additional upside continuation. When a little correction appears on the lower time frame, a trade to the upside is started when it is broken. This idea is very effective because it uses the predictable momentum from the lower time frame to feed into the momentum of the higher time frame. In chapter 7, you will discover the precise entry requirements for this and other trades..

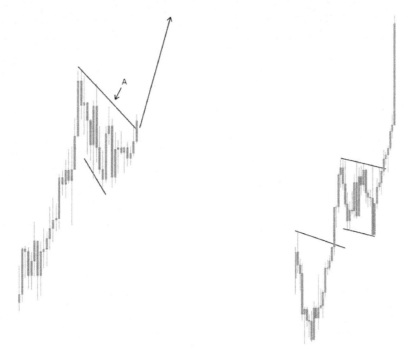

Image 3.39: The daily chart is displayed on the chart to the left. As price exits the correction (A) preceding the initial impulse, the structure predicts additional upward price continuance. The 1-hour chart is to the right. Just after the HTF break, a small, slightly falling correction provided a definite entry point that would not have been possible on the HTF. A great application of multiple time frame analysis is to combine the smaller pattern on the lower time frame with a bigger-picture bias from a higher time frame..

The 15-minute Chart: Additional Entries

The shortest time window we'll utilize is the 15-minute chart. I used to only trade using the 1-hour time frame as my entrance time frame, but I discovered that using the 15-minute time period allowed me to uncover more trades that may have been concealed or at least disguised in the 1-hour time frame. This is most helpful when there is rapid intraday movement in the markets. Examine the picture below.

Image 3.40: With a downside bias, the EUR/GBP is trading inside of a corrective channel. On the hourly chart, there is a significant downward impulse and a 2-candle pullback (A). But since there is no obvious structure or pattern with clear entry and departure points, there is no entry on this time frame. The 15-minute chart fills that role..

Image 3.41: The story told by the 15-minute chart is substantially different. Examine the variations between the areas designated A on the two charts. On the 15-minute, what appears to be just 2 candles on the hour is actually a bear flag. The particulars of this configuration are covered in chapter 7. There

are instances when trade opportunities on the 15-minute are as evident as those on the 1-hour..

15-Minute Chart: Refining Structures

The 15-minute chart can be used in a second method to provide clarity and richness that the 1-hour time frame could lack. The 15-minute chart can be carefully and expertly analyzed to provide traders with information on patterns and structures on the 1-hour chart. Consider it a secondary filter that can be applied to improve 1-hour structures that can appear underdeveloped. Look at the illustration in figure 3.40 below:

Image 3.42: USD/CAD makes an abrupt downward movement before correcting sideways. This graph displays the correction as it was during the preceding hour. It is challenging to detect touches and identify accurate entry and exit points due to the compressed price action.

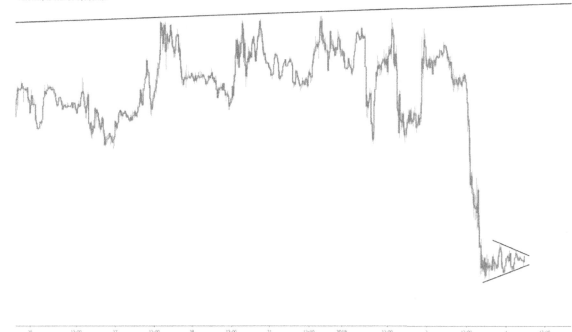

Image 3.43: The same pattern is depicted in this figure, but from the standpoint of a 15-minute chart.

We can design a much more precise structure using this chart's much clearer pattern and identified touched points. An intelligent trader who utilized the 15-minute chart properly could have placed himself into a volatile trade that would have produced substantial percentage winnings

MTF Analysis: Summary

One of the most crucial elements in technical trading is the efficient correlation and use of several time frames. However, the ideas we have covered so far must be internalized on a subconscious level in order to properly comprehend them and employ them to their best advantage. It will take diligent study and regular exposure to the course material to achieve this. However, when dissected at the micro level, the fundamental ideas and lessons of multiple time frame analysis are actually relatively straightforward but extremely useful:

• Never dig down to the smaller time frames first; always start with the larger ones.

• In comparison to smaller time frames, higher time frames have more structurally significant structures.

• We will employ lower time frame continuation patterns to locate significant entry points that take advantage of impulsive movements in the higher time frames.

• Our longer-term directional bias is dependent on whether a higher time frame's corrected condition is an ascending channel or a descending channel.

• Even with a higher time frame correction, there may be numerous trade chances. In reality, price moves within the higher time frame correction might occur on a number of lower time frame impulsive legs, providing straightforward continuation trades.

• When pricing on the HTF is moving impulsively, lower time frame patterns that indicate a directional move in the opposite direction frequently fail due to the higher time frame momentum taking over.

• It's crucial to avoid developing a directional bias from the lower time frames because there is more noise and volatility there. LTFs are merely used as entry points; all trades are based on the higher time frame structure.

   • • Never zoom in to fix the problem of competing time frames; instead, move further away and take a broader view of what is happening. Use the shorter time frames only after that to manage your market entry..

The Sum is Greater Than Its Parts

Simple pattern recognition is a skill used by new traders and has very little real trading utility when taken out of its proper context, as I stated in one of the previous sections of this chapter. Then, I introduced you to each of the specific elements that will give you the technical expertise to advance above and beyond the analytical capabilities of beginning traders: the examination of the two main price movements, impulses and corrections; a comprehension of natural progression to forecast, for lack of a better term, probable price direction; the steps to identify and depict pertinent market structures; and, finally, the nuances of multiple time frame analysis. Although there will never be a technical analysis holy grail, this assemblage of historically validated technical patterns in a multiple time frame setting comes very near. These elements can be used skillfully to create a trading framework where the whole is significantly bigger than the sum of its parts.

After going over everything you learned in this chapter, think about how it might affect your trade. If you understood how to predict market direction from the recognition of basic structures, how do you think your trading would change? If you were aware that a potential inflection point marked the beginning of the downturn, how would you manage your trades differently? What effect would eliminating trades with low quality through your knowledge of numerous time frame analysis have on your bottom line? I hope this chapter has sparked a lot of thought in you..

Trader Action Points

- • When it comes to making trading judgments, there are two schools of thought: technical analysis and fundamental analysis.

- • There are two types of price movements: impulsive and corrective.

- • Impulses are distinct price movements that have a very clear directional bias and can travel in either an upwards or a downward direction.

- • Price channels that are choppy during corrections often exhibit back-and-forth price movement that can be ascending, declining, or sideways.

- • As a result, there are 5 conceivable price movements: an impulse move up or down, a correction move up or down, or a sideways correction.

- • The market's propensity to move in a sequence of predictable steps based on the current structure is referred to as "natural progression."

- • One of the most crucial instruments in technical trading is the efficient correlation and use of several time frames.

CHAPTER 4 - RISK MANAGEMENT

Paul Tudor Jones once said, "I am constantly worried about losing money rather than making money."

I agonized over whether to include this chapter before the specific trading setups for a very long time. After learning about market structure and price activity, wouldn't it make sense to start with the trading techniques themselves? Or how about getting a handle on trade psychology first? Despite their importance, I thought it was time to move on to what I consider to be the next most significant aspect of trading. I wanted the chapters to be organized logically, with a smooth transition from one trading theory to the next and room for a steady accumulation of skills and information. Risk management will therefore take precedence over all other activities because a trader's primary responsibility is to safeguard his capital.

The goal of this chapter is to provide the reader with useful, applicable tools for managing risk in a variety of markets by delving deeply into the theoretical and practical consequences of risk management. I begin by discussing the significance of managing our per-trade risk using strategic stop loss placement and position size tools. Then, I explain what I like to refer to as the 1% rule and examine the statistical disadvantages faced by traders who allow their accounts to experience drawdowns. The chapter then moves on to other risk management issues that a lot of retail traders frequently forget about. We will talk about asset correlation as well as total portfolio risk. No matter where you are in your trading adventure or development, it is critical that we set up sound risk management guidelines today so that we can go on to the later stages of your education. Therefore, carefully consider its concepts since this chapter may be one of the most crucial in the entire book..

Why Risk Management is King

If you were to look at traders who had lost all of their money, you would discover that a large portion of their trading issues were due to inadequate risk management. Many of these traders would have failed to properly manage the risk in their deals since they were so intent on exponentially expanding their profits. They neglected to mention a fundamental trading principle: managing risk in deals and letting the market handle gains are the trader's responsibilities, not trying to "make" money on the markets. Although we as traders have no control over the markets, we can determine how much risk to take on each deal. The profits will take care of themselves as long as we join our trades at high-probability entry points, manage our risk exposure, and quit when our trade has become invalidated.

Based on my observations of failing traders, taking on too much risk is the single biggest cause of trading failure. By permitting one or two exorbitant losses to significantly deplete weeks or months' worth of trading earnings, a trader who has no understanding of risk management might seriously ruin their account.

Psychologists found that participants' psychological reactions to losses were twice as powerful as their psychological reactions to profits in a series of games where there was a chance of money gains or losses. This is why many traders who experience one or two losses frequently proceed to commit a series of risky trading mistakes, such as "revenge trading," which typically results in additional losses and creates a self-fulfilling prophecy whereby the inevitable result is a blown account and another unsuccessful trader in the poor house.

The quotation from Paul Tudor Jones that began this chapter stated that he always considers his potential losses before considering the potential gains from his transactions. He was able to rigorously limit his risk to establish a lengthy and lucrative trading career by compulsively focusing on his risk exposure, becoming a trading legend in the process. Consistent traders play excellent defense rather than offense by putting risk first..

Initial Risk and Position Sizing

In trading, there aren't many unchanging truths. The majority of trading rules are often flexible and subject to many different trading techniques. However, there is one trading maxim that has endured the test of time: minimize your losses. Which of our trades will generate profits and which will generate losses cannot ever be predicted in advance. Profits and losses can be distributed in a way that seems random, as we'll look at in the later chapter on practical psychology. Therefore, it's crucial that we make sure our maximum risk is kept low in every transaction we make, low enough to guarantee that we play the game for a long enough time to experience the positive expectation of our edge..

Risk Per Trade: The 1% Rule

Let's begin by establishing the most fundamental principle of risk management: how much risk to allocate to each trade. We can maintain calm and concentration on carrying out our trading strategy by placing modest bets on each trade. It's easy to carry out this. The percentage of the account balance that we consistently risk in each trade is fixed at 1%. This is what I refer to as the 1% rule. I'll tell it again: the amount of money we risk in any trade is set at 1% of the account balance, which is a constant percentage. Let's say you have $10,000 in your trading account. Your total loss on any trade will not exceed £100 or 1%. Your risk would be 1% of your account balance, or £540 each trade, if it were £54,000. It's crucial to remember that while the financial risk will fluctuate as the account balance changes, the percentage amount will always stay the same.

Let's revisit the initial illustration with an account with £10,000. Let's say you have a healthy percentage return of 10% at the end of the month. The new balance on your account going into the following month is £11,000. Due to the fact that £110 is 1% of £11,000, your risk per trade will now be £110. The percentage in relation to the account amount may be higher even though you are taking on more financial risk.

Many novice traders may find it difficult to comprehend this fundamental principle because they think their ability to place large deals will be constrained. The 1% rule does not impose any restrictions on how much of your trading capital you can use for trading. This means that no lost deal will cause your account balance to decrease by more than 1%. I'd even venture to argue that the 1% rule is one of the best trading guidelines one could come up with. When you're only risking 1% per trade, it's difficult to blow up an account or to suffer a major, emotional, and financial downturn. Even with 5 consecutive losing trades, the loss would only be 5%, which is not emotionally unstable and is simple to recover from with a few strong profitable trades.

For a trader who has recently had three consecutive loss trades, think about the 1% rule. The account balance is down 3%, but since your average reward to risk ratio for each trade is 3:1, this is not a significant concern. Compare that to another trader who takes a 5% risk on each transaction. He's had a similar run of three losses, but his account is down a startling 15%! Do you believe he will be able to maintain his composure in the face of such a significant drawdown? What action do you anticipate he will take? The majority of the time, such severe account damage is the consequence of a series of expensive trading mistakes; common emotional responses include overtrading and failing to close out losing positions in the hopes of a comeback. The plain truth is that significant losses color our perspective of the world and distort our objective reality as we become frantic to find what we've lost. Small losses help us maintain objectivity so that we may concentrate on following ethical trading practices and flawlessly carrying out our trading strategy..

Position Sizing

Position sizing is how we make sure our trade risk is restricted to 1%. Position sizing is simply the number of stock shares or currency units we buy or sell in a trade. My position size in that trade is 125 shares if I execute a trade in which I acquire 125 shares of Facebook stock. So how can we precisely calculate the size of each position? Position size calculation is a by-product of three factors:

what market are you trading?

Depending on the product being traded, different markets have different methods for sizing positions. For example, stock transactions are defined by the number of shares you buy or sell short, whereas forex trades are measured by the amount of currency being bought or sold short.

What you're risking (the 1% rule) on that trade

You must first determine how much risk you are willing to take on this specific position before you can determine the size of the position. You are aware that our risk for each trade should always be 1% of the account amount. There will be times when this is upped to 2% when using my risk pyramiding method (which you'll learn about in chapter 6).

*Simply divide your capital by 100 to get 1%, which is the amount of money you will be risking in this trade, and this is what 1% of your account capital translates to.

how far the entrance price is from the stop loss price

We can determine the risk per unit by calculating the difference between the entrance price of the trade and the stop loss price. Purchasing a stock for $50 per share and setting a stop loss at $48 would be a straightforward example. We have a $2 risk per share if we subtract the entrance price of 50 from the stop price of 48. Our per-unit risk is as follows. Simply divide the risk per unit by the overall account risk to determine the position size. This reveals the total number of units (shares) we are able to purchase without going beyond our risk tolerance. Let's go over a straightforward practice case to assist make this clear. I'll use a stock trade as an illustration of the fundamental ideas in this case.

You want to risk 1% of your trading account's $50,000 total (£500) on the following transaction. You choose to go long and place your stop loss at £8 on a stock that is now trading at £10 per share. Your per-unit risk, or the total risk you are assuming for each unit of stock you are buying in that trade, is the difference between the entry price of £10 and the stop loss price of £8. You divide your per-unit risk by the £500 total deal risk to determine how many shares to purchase to execute this trade. £2 times £500 equals 250 shares. If your stop loss price is reached after you have entered this trade and the deal is closed out, you will lose £2 per share, which when multiplied by 250 shares results in a loss of £500.

1% of the account balance divided by the per-unit risk is the trade size.

Forex Position Sizing

It's crucial to keep in mind that position sizing in currency trading differs differently from that in stock trading. This is due to the fact that fluctuations in forex prices are measured in tiny price changes between two currencies' exchange rates, or "pips." To determine the position size in forex, we must first determine the importance of each pip to the transaction. I won't lie; it's a far more difficult procedure than stock sizing, one that can also be perplexing. Fortunately, using online position sizing calculators makes the procedure quick and easy. All you need is a few details about the deal you want to make. The calculator will instantly tell you how many units of currency you will need to buy or sell in order to stay within your predefined risk parameters. All you need to do is enter the size of your account balance, the risk percentage you wish to take in this trade (which is, as you know, 1%), the size of your stop loss in pips, and the currency your account is funded in. How easy to use and time-saving these calculators are is demonstrated in Image 4.1 below. For URL addresses to the position sizing calculator I use, see the resources section..

Position Size Calculator

Values

Account currency	GBP ▼	Required
Account size	100000	Required
Risk Ratio, %	1	Required Switch to Money
Stop-Loss, pips	30	required
Currency pair	EURUSD ▼	Required
Current (GBPUSD) Ask price :	1.21925	

Calculate

Results

Money , GBP	£1000.00
Units	406417
Lots	4.064

Image 4.1: Calculator for sizing forex positions. Simply enter the pair being traded, the size of your trading account, the risk percentage you desire to take, the currency your account is funded in, and the size of the stop loss in pips. The calculator will instantly inform you of the maximum number of units you can buy or sell without going above your specified risk threshold. For immediate access, enter the URL into your browser. Alternatively, visit the Resources section at the book's end..

Expressing Results as a Ratio of Initial Risk

The R multiple, which we may describe as a ratio of our original risk when we first enter a trade, allows us to express all profits and losses as a percentage of that risk. Many traders will find it advantageous to begin looking at all of their transactions' P&L in terms of the R multiple.

Consider that you opened a position and staked 1% of your account equity on it. Your starting risk in this trade is £720 based on your £72000 account, which is denoted by the letter R (short for risk). This would be a -1R loss if your stop loss was to be activated. The loss would therefore be equal to the initial risk you assumed when you entered the deal. This would be a +2R trade if the deal developed to the point where the profit was equal to twice the initial risk, or £1440. The amount of money you initially risked would have been more than doubled in profit. Operating in R multiples relieves much of the emotional stress we experience when considering the actual monetary amounts, making it a useful tool for both novice and experienced traders. As a novice trader, one of my major problems was continuously comparing my gains and losses to actual monetary situations, such as "I just lost the equivalent of four PT sessions" or "I just made enough to cover my rent in one day." I discovered the hard way that seasoned traders are considerably more prone to view their gains and losses as a reflection of the initial risk than as a simple sum of cold, hard cash. The psychological effects of a trader risking £100 each transaction compared to one risking £10,000 per trade could be very different. However, describing these sums in terms of the R multiple can help the traders view them with a certain level of objectivity if both amounts equal the same proportion of their respective trading balances.

Portfolio Risk overall

After establishing guidelines for our risk in specific transactions, we must decide how much total risk we are ready to take on at any given time for the entire account. While we already have a 1% risk running in another position, it's possible that numerous high-quality transactions will come around. Unfortunately, neither does the market care if you already have open positions; neither does it wait around to offer good trading opportunities. It will be less difficult to make impulsive and emotional trading judgments if you are prepared for these situations in advance and have clear regulations in place.

Our overall exposure rule shields us from any string of losses, whereas the 1% rule shields you from catastrophic losses in any one position. When several trading chances present themselves, its enforcement prevents us from overcommitting monetarily and compel us to be more discriminating in selecting and executing only the best setups. Implementing these two guidelines will be like having a personal risk manager who will keep an eye on you at all times and keep you safe in this possible financial minefield.

I am a cautious trader. Your trading rules should reflect your personality and style, which is a frequent concept in this book and a belief I strongly adhere to. Your preference for risk is also included in this. For this reason, I base my trading on a 3% overall portfolio risk guideline. I use 3% since one of the criteria I'll look for when I analyze a possible trade is the transaction having at least a 3:1 reward to risk ratio. In that transaction, I want the possible reward to be at least three times greater than the potential loss, ideally much more. As a result, if I have three open positions, each of which hits its own 1% loss point, I know that I can recoup and return to breakeven with just one reliable 3:1 deal. This benefits my psychological state. Keep in mind that the 3% limitation only applies to risk, not the total amount of trades we can execute simultaneously. My 3% account barrier will be met if I execute 3 trades on the same day, each with a 1% active risk. However, even though I still have three open positions, if I move the stop to the BE point and reduce the risk from one of these trades, I only have 2% of open risk. I currently have 1% of risk that I can use if another trade opportunity arises.

The 3% portfolio risk threshold regularly adjusts based on the fluctuating value of the account balance, just like the 1% rule. With no active positions from the previous month and a trading equity of £50,000, your maximum risk per transaction is £500, while your maximum overall risk is £1500. Your new permitted 3% overall risk exposure is now £1545 (3% of £51500) if you were to execute a trade that produced a 3R profit of £1500 and your new account balance was £51500.

You might think that 3% is too low, too cautious, or too safe. If you naturally take on more risk than 3% with your trading, that is acceptable. There isn't a universal solution to this. The response that is best for you is the only correct response. Some traders I know are at ease taking on open risk exposure of up to 6–10%. However, you must take the worst-case situation into account before choosing what is best for you. Consider what would happen if you opened many positions, increasing your risk exposure to the fullest. Imagine that all of those transactions simultaneously reached their designated stop loss levels. Will you feel at ease with a 6% account hit in a single day? Suppose 10%? What future psychological effects do you anticipate that would have? I never get emotionally invested in the results of any series of trades, so I keep my overall account risk low. It doesn't matter to me if I place 3 trades that day and they are all stopped out. My emotional sensor isn't even close to picking up on the 3% hit. But a 7% hit in a single day? I'm not going to like that at all. The more fuel you pour into the emotional fire that is risk, the greater and deadlier the fire will become as a result..

The Mathematical Realities of Drawdown

You ought to have two risk management guidelines in place by this time. The 1% rule, which restricts your risk exposure across all trades, is the first. The portfolio exposure rule, which limits your risk across the entire account, is the second. Yet why? Why should traders pay so close attention to risk? You've heard the idea explaining why it's nearly hard to become a successful trader without having a strong desire to avoid taking on too much risk. You are aware that one of the primary causes of trader failure is the inability to limit losses, which causes a few losses to cause serious account damage. The value of risk management, however, has not yet been supported by mathematics. In the following sentences, I want to help you understand risk in a more theoretical and in-depth way. I'll demonstrate the mathematical facts of downturn and how your odds of a successful recovery are exponentially reduced for every additional percentage point you lose.

Imagine you make a series of terrible, high-risk trades and lose 50% of your account balance. What percentage return must you obtain to return to breakeven? If you're like most individuals, 50% will be your first thought. But you would be mistaken. wrong in every way. In reality, to get back to breakeven, you would need a 100% return on the cash that is still available. In other words, you would need to quadruple your remaining balance to break even after losing half of your account balance. And the exponential nature of this mathematical fact. Look over the table below. To make up for a 10% loss, you would need to make an 11% profit. However, a 25% loss would necessitate a 33% gain to return you to your starting position. Keep in mind that the gain needed to recoup grows higher with each small increase in drawdown. A further 50% required gain is needed to recover from a 50% loss as opposed to a 60% loss. Even a 10% increase in loss results in an additional 50% of profit being needed to make up for it. Because of this, risk management is crucial. By applying the 1% rule, even a run of five losses will only cause a 5% drawdown, which is scarcely appreciable account harm. Think about even 10 defeats. You place 10 deals, each with 1% risk exposure, and all of them lose all of their money up front. I can tell with certainty that it is extremely rare that with the five trade settings you will learn later, you will experience a run of 10 straight losses. But suppose you had an extremely nasty hand by accident. Sure, that 10% decline is probably going to stir up some feelings. But is it an unrecoverable, financially destabilizing event? Actually, no. Not that it's simple to generate the 11% needed to cover the loss, but it won't be the end of your trading career either, is what I'm trying to imply. When you only need an 11% gain to recoup in the extremely improbable scenario that you make 10 consecutive losing trades, you know your risk management strategy is effective..

Loss %	% Gain required to recover
1	1
5	5.3
10	11
25	33

50	100
60	150

Image 4.2: The drawdown's mathematical realities. The required percentage gain for various drawdown levels is shown in the table. Take note of how the amount needed to return to breakeven becomes exponential as the loss grows. Due to this, strict risk management is crucial..

Correlation

The differences we have made regarding risk thus far are all related to one common idea: losing money. The most obvious and substantial risk we take on while trading is, of course, this one. There is one more thing to think about, though, before this chapter is over: asset correlation. Simply put, correlation is the propensity for specific assets to move together. There are nevertheless very substantial ramifications for active traders who plan to maintain many positions, even if those positions are only to be held for hours or days, even though correlation is a more major problem for the longer-term investor when building a portfolio. Traders who are unaware of the effects of correlations may unintentionally overexpose their funds.

How few traders are aware of correlation's impacts and how they affect risk management never ceases to amaze me. As short-term traders, many of these traders completely disregard correlations, believing that the only factors influencing whatever transactions they are now executing are the supply and demand dynamics exclusive to specific markets. This idea is at best incorrect and at worst harmful to your finances. Yes, the market's dynamics of buying and selling determine prices. However, no market trades independently of itself in a vacuum. Large capital pools will typically move in tandem. Consider Brexit-related news that weakens the pound. Not just in the pairings of one or two isolated currencies, but likely across the board, the GBP will begin to decline. Or think about stocks. US stock movement can be traced to the sector and larger overall index it is a part of for about 75% of the time. Unaware of the consequences of correlation, a stock trader holding five large-capitalization technology stocks may assume he is risking 5% of his account on these positions, but it would be more accurate to conceive of him as risking 5% on a single trade. Most traders would consider a 5% risk in a single trade to be completely unacceptable, yet many do so when they unintentionally start positions that are closely connected. The picture below demonstrates correlation in use..

Image 4.3: action of correlation. The chart on the left displays the GBP/USD 1-hour time frame, while the chart on the right displays the GBP/JPY 1-hour time frame for the same time period. The graphs appear to be very similar..

Take a minute to think about your maximum account exposure limit and determine whether you would feel at ease taking that much risk in a single trade. There is a potential that all three of your active trades will move simultaneously if they all involve the same currency and make a significant move. While you may believe that you are managing trades in three separately moving pairings, each with 1% risk, in actuality, you are actually managing 3% of the risk on only one currency. I once went to a trading meetup in my hometown and talked to several other young traders who were in a similar stage of development to me. Just one person, let's name him Harry was describing to me how he lost his entire month's earnings in a single day through a string of unsuccessful trades. While it was undoubtedly unpleasant to erase a month's worth of work in a single day, he claimed that the most important thing was that the four lost trades were all valid setups. Even more, he commented on how 'very hilarious' it was that every setting was so similar to the others. I requested the trading pairs he has used: AUD/USD, USD/CAD, USD/JPY, and USD/CHF in an effort to provide constructive criticism regarding his trading. Poor Harry had staked money on four pairs with US dollar effect. Additionally, he had executed these trades on the day when the crucial Non-Farm Payroll figures were supposed to be revealed. Before he could move anything to breakeven, the numbers were revealed, and the USD fell, tagging his stops on each trade. The positions had all initially risen in his favor. By making a rookie trading mistake, this individual lost a month's worth of gains in just one day, yet he was still proud of himself! Harry didn't realize the folly of his trading mistake until I explained that the setups appeared so similar because they were all pairings denominated in USD and that they were quite likely to move together. He has committed two significant risk management mistakes. In addition to disregarding correlation entirely, he also chose to execute these transactions prior to a large, high-impact, market-moving news announcement. He would have avoided this wholly avoidable trading sin if he had an efficient decision-making procedure in place, one that took into account all the many aspects of the transaction (such as if there were news releases) before entering. Learning the elements that make up a successful entry into the market is the topic of the following chapter.

And just in case you're curious, Harry is doing OK. After the meetup, we remained in touch and continued to talk about trading strategies. He hasn't yet made the same error..

Conclusion

We've just looked at the idea of risk and the useful tools that traders can use to stay away from costly financial mistakes that could endanger their trading accounts. We've looked at the mathematical implications of different drawdown percentages and how applying risk management guidelines like the 1% rule and setting up an absolute account risk exposure rule will assist safeguard your account from irreparable harm and decline. You should now be completely prepared with a risk management framework using the rules and recommendations in this chapter, which will serve as the basis for placing trades using the elements we will learn about in the following three chapters.

Investor Action Points

• The first and most crucial task for a skilled trader is risk management. First and foremost, we should work to reduce the amount of risk we take on in each trade and across the board.

• Risk management, not trying to turn a profit, is the trader's responsibility. If a trader uses a trading strategy with a statistical advantage, earnings will take care of themselves by putting risk first.

• Start applying the 1% rule right now, never putting more than 1% of your account at risk in a single deal.

• The total amount of risk exposure you are willing to take on across all of your positions at any given moment is your personal portfolio risk rule, which you should develop. Think about the psychological and emotional effects of breaking your rule. How will you be feeling? What future psychological effects do you anticipate that would have? If a trader wants to develop a successful risk management system, they must confront these issues head-on. The more gasoline you pour on the fire that is your emotional condition, the greater and deadlier the fire will become. Keep this in mind.

- • When a trader has many open positions, asset correlation is a crucial but sometimes disregarded feature. 5 positions with high correlation, each with 1% open risk, equates to 5% risk exposure in one market. Understanding how those markets tend to move together is crucial if you plan to hold various assets. As a general rule, FX pairings with a same currency and stocks from the same industry sector are likely to exhibit some degree of association..

CHAPTER 5 – ENTRING THE MARKET

"Key components of trading and investing are entry and exit points. That should be said again. Trading and investing require precise entry and exit points. Why would you ever buy a stock at the incorrect time, whether you are swing trading, day trading, or a long-term investor? Unfortunately, there are a lot of market players who do it every day without any formal training. F. McAllen

It would definitely be helpful at this point to quickly review the ground we have already covered. It's crucial that you comprehend the principles' chronological order as well as the rationale behind their organizational design. I would assume that many readers are anxious to start utilizing the trading setups right away because they feel they are ready to do so, but doing so would not be beneficial. Each and every element of the strategy must be grasped and internalized before understanding the setups because they serve as the building blocks around which these trades are built.

We examine each component of entering the market in this chapter. As we explore the potential influence of news and briefly go through each of the important events traders should be aware of, we will first focus on the two entry types that are used in the five trade settings. Consider the knowledge we gain from this the warm-up to a rigorous workout. A high-intensity circuit training routine wouldn't be started without first going through the appropriate warm-up exercises, such as pulse rising and mobility work. Before diving into the intense workout that is trading setups, the information in this chapter serves as each reader's personal warm-up.

entries ARE crucial

The common belief that entrance is "the least important part of the trade" has always amazed me about so many trading books. In order to support their argument, authors typically go on to say that proper position sizing, risk management, and sound psychology all take precedence over certain entry criteria. Some even assert that the entry strategy can practically be arbitrary because effective risk management will enable you to profit from profitable trades to the point where the gains will outweigh the losses.

Please do not misunderstand what I am saying here; all of those things are very important, but to say that the entry is the least important part of a trade is equivalent to saying that pedaling is the least important part of riding a bike; the pedaling part is undoubtedly insignificant in comparison to the skillful balancing of the bike and the cognitive awareness needed to ride safely.

This flawed reasoning downplays the importance of actually having a tried-and-true trading technique. The exact entry trigger is a part of the trading process, even though it isn't the end-all, be-all of a great trading career. Even if a trader manages his risk exposure carefully and has a great attitude toward trading, it's doubtful that he will produce consistent gains without technical expertise. Consider this. Would you agree that more traders would succeed if trading were as simple as managing risk and then letting gains outweigh losses? I've worked with traders who DO manage risk, DO make average gains that outweigh their losses, and DO have great dispositions, but if their technical proficiency is lacking, they will still struggle to produce consistent returns. The majority of these traders engage in the maddening "breakeven dance," when one or two months of gains are counterbalanced by one or two months of losses.

A strong trading strategy starts with a decent entry point even though it doesn't necessarily stop there.

Two is preferable to one.

There are two ways that we might start our trading and enter the market. These entry kinds will be referred to as Type 1 and Type 2. In a moment, we will look deeper into the two entry kinds. But first, let's address the question of why two?

The majority of trading techniques use one type of entry, which is often split into two categories: breakouts and reversals. One of these entry types serves as the foundation for almost all trading systems, regardless of the precise technical criteria they employ to locate and execute trades. Consider the straightforward range trading strategy that trades the reversal as price approaches support and resistance levels or any of the variants of the traditional breakout trading methods, which all employ a major price breakout as their primary entry signal. When it comes to the actual moment of entry, even pullback strategies—the classic techniques for capitalizing on trending markets—all involve some kind of reversal criteria. These algorithms tend to overlook numerous potentially profitable trading chances since the market must meet very particular requirements before a transaction can be justified. As a result, they only consider one sort of entry. However, the market offers us multiple opportunities to profit by utilizing two modes of entry.

Let's use an example to illustrate.

Trader on the Breakout:

A breakout of the range in the direction of the trend on a higher time frame is what the breakout trader watches for during periods of price consolidation. In order to be entered into the trade should price successfully break out, he will put his entry order above the range (or below in the event of a short). Now weigh the advantages and disadvantages of this entry strategy. The benefits include a degree of trade confirmation provided by waiting for the breakout to occur, as well as directional bias confirmation provided by price behavior that continues outside of the expected range. Additionally, he guards against a pattern failure because if price trades against his forecast and in the opposite direction, he will not have suffered a loss because his order would not have been filled. Putting the entry order in such a way that the price must commit to the projected direction is equivalent to protection against being tagged into trades that aren't already headed in his direction. However, there are disadvantages to this kind of admission. He will almost certainly enter the trade late and risk missing high-probability entry opportunities in the structure before the breakout if he waits for the breakout to happen. The Type 1 method is the breakout entrance.

Trader Reversals

Alternatively, the price's actual reversal might be used as the following price action-based entry strategy. We take a position in expectation that this is the point at which price will reverse, rather than waiting for price to commit to itself by moving in our way. The majority of trading systems employ this entry strategy at crucial levels of support and resistance because they offer definite moments at which a reversal is likely to occur. Imagine a structure similar to the one in the previous example, where price fluctuated erratically in one direction before settling in a corrective range. Assume that the bottom and top of this pattern contain distinct contact points that allow us to determine its form. The reversal trader can use candlestick reversal patterns to craft an entry precisely at the base of the structure, anticipating that price would reverse at these levels once more and then trade back up to the range's resistance level. By joining the trade early, he will already be positioned should price break from the structure. He can still turn a profit playing the range, though, should the price stay fixed in the range. The main advantage of the reverse procedure is this. You could be able to position yourself into an explosive move at a very opportune region with a terrific reward to risk if a reversal is completed in alignment with the higher time frame momentum. Although reversal trades typically carry a somewhat lower overall strike rate than breakout trades since there is less certainty that price will move in the desired direction, they do tend to provide better reward to risk prospects. Our Type 2 entry strategy is the reversal trade.

Trader Hybrid

Imagine a trader who employs a hybrid strategy, allowing him to switch between the two entry options and take advantage of various deals as they become available on the market. He consistently makes use of both rather than waiting for the market to always offer the ideal circumstances and requirements for one form of entry. When the price reaches the third touch point on a structure with two distinct touch points, it can be interpreted as a reversal (Type 2). Then, if price breaks the structure successfully and produces a continuation pattern, the particular setup can be profited from by applying a Type 1 breakout. Opportunities that would otherwise be hidden from other trading styles utilizing only one are unlocked by two entry types..

Image 5.1: Clear illustrations of Type 1 and Type 2 entry techniques. Price refused the third touch of the rising channel, which led to the initial entry, which was a Type 2 reversal. The trade was entered into on the grounds that it was likely that the price would move toward the channel's bottom and maybe break. After the initial breakout, price created a straightforward flag continuation pattern, which led to the second entry, the Type 1. If the structure had completely broken to the downside, the trade would have been opened. Numerous techniques with only one entrance system would have a constrained ability to generate income. With two distinct entry strategies at our disposal, we can profit from a variety of trade opportunities as they arise in the market..

Here's an overview of the entry types:

Type 1: Of the two entry types, this one is more frequent. Entry happens at the point where the particular structure being exchanged breaks. There are two major advantages to entering the trade during the break. The first is that we don't have to actively monitor the markets because we may set our entry orders in advance. To "set it and forget it," we can simply enter our orders based on the precise pattern being traded. The benefit of confirmation is the second benefit of this entry type. Price would have had to have moved in the anticipated trade direction before the structure was broken, confirming our directional bias. Type 1 entries can be strategically placed with stop loss orders to enter smaller continuation patterns like Bull and Bear Flags as well as the breakouts of larger corrective formations..

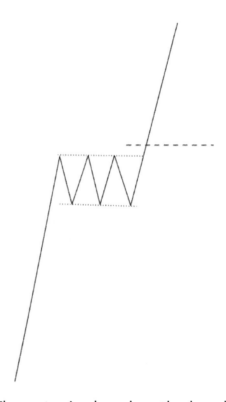

Image 5.2: Type 1 entry. The entry is placed on the break of the structure. The trade will only be executed if price successfully breaks the pattern. The dotted line shows the level the entry order would be set.

Type 2: This entry is made more forcefully, and the exchange is made inside the structure's walls. We are entering from within the pattern in anticipation of the breakout rather than waiting for it to break. Since Type 2s occur before the anticipated breakout actually occurs, they are often riskier because the setup being traded can only be confirmed after the breakout has taken place. However, Type 2 entries can offer us more lucrative trades when they are in line with the higher time frame structure since we can typically enter them with a tighter stop loss, delivering a higher reward to risk ratio and capturing more of the move by entering sooner..

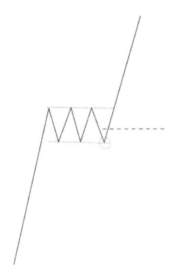

Image 5.3: entry of type 2. While the price is still confined within the structure or pattern being traded, the entrance is interpreted as a reversal. The level where the ingress would happen is indicated by the dotted line.

Remember that neither of the two entry kinds is necessarily superior than the other. Depending on the trader's personality and trading style, either entry can be leveraged to offer multiple opportunities to join the market. As a more cautious trader, I prefer to wait for a specific amount of price confirmation before initiating a trade, and I only enter Type 2 trades when several confluence factors are present and the transaction is aligned with the higher time frame structure..

Basic Candlestick Patterns

There are two requirements for Type 2 entries. The first is the setting and how it relates to price movement. In the following chapter, you will discover where and when to take Type 2s. The second criterion indicates that a real reversal in this sector is probably taking place. We must ensure that price is truly reversing, not only because it is in a likely reversal area. The use of candlestick patterns allows for this. Candlestick patterns and formations have a variety of intricately labeled patterns, making them perhaps a separate field of study unto themselves. In the educational literature, terms like shooting stars, dojis, hammers, and abandoned newborns are only a few examples. Fortunately, we only need a few simple patterns to help us time entering the market and verify that our Type 2 entry is in fact a high-probability reversal moment. There are two fundamental patterns, each with a bullish or negative mood, giving rise to a total of four potential patterns. Please be aware that a Type 2 entry can only be accepted if one of these candlestick patterns is present. Because they will serve as your triggers for any Type 2 setup, you must master these patterns before moving on to actual trading settings..

High test:
a bearish candlestick with a short body that is close to the candle's low and a long upper wick. It shows that even if price was able to increase significantly during the session, sellers were able to seize control and drive price close to the candle's open, signaling a negative move is likely..

Image 5.4: A high-test candle.

Low test:
a bullish candlestick that is close to the candle's height and has a long lower wick. While price was able to fall dramatically during the session, buyers were able to seize control and drive price back up to close to the candle's open, signaling that an up move is likely..

Image 5.5: A low-test candle.

Bearish engulfing:

This pattern develops when a larger bullish candlestick from the previous period is completely engulfed by a bearish candlestick. The pattern signals probable selling pressure because it shows that the sellers were able to decrease the price below the preceding candle's open..

Image 5.6: Bearish engulfing pattern.

Bullish engulfing:

This pattern develops when a larger bearish candlestick from the previous period is completely engulfed by a bullish candlestick. The pattern suggests that buyers were able to push the price higher than the preceding candle's open, indicating possible purchasing pressure..

Image 5.7: Bullish engulfing pattern.

News

As technical traders, we rarely use fundamental data when making trading decisions. To prevent being caught in intraday volatility or possibly explosive, irregular price noise, however, market-moving news events and scheduled economic data releases must be taken into account. Due to the currency markets' propensity for volatile and unexpected price behavior around high-impact news releases, forex traders should exercise extra caution when dealing with these announcements. In the run-up to these releases, forex brokers also frequently tend to raise spreads, which could result in you being tagged into and out of trades early, even if the price didn't reach your exact exit point. A recent example of market volatility triggered by news is shown in image 5.8 below..

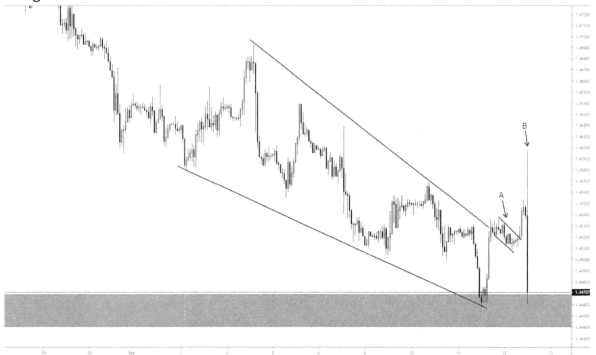

Image 5.8: After price suddenly breaks a corrective channel, EUR/CAD displays a traditional Bull Flag (A). The trade initially proceeds as expected, with a powerful break to the upside. However, a press conference remark from the European Central Bank causes tremendous volatility, leading a price spike up and then a sharp drop, retracing the entire prior gain and more.

The volatile candle at B created in a matter of approximately 5 minutes, however you can't see it on this time frame; this is a significant level of volatility for such a brief period. Traders who had taken the long position on the Flag's break might have suffered losses greater than 1R. The stop order might not have been able to be executed at the desired price due to the rapid and turbulent market movement. To avoid many such disappointing losses, it would be advisable to keep up with news on any of the currencies you plan to trade. A trader entering the market without knowledge of them is neither doing so safely nor sensibly..

I joined a trading group of about 1000 traders, mostly male and female traders from the UK, when I was learning about the markets throughout my formative years. Their plan was entirely based on the data from the charts. Longer-term fundamental factors and current affairs, it was thought, were immaterial because price would always abide by and respect the technical frameworks in which it was trading. This disregard for fundamental knowledge can be expensive, as was demonstrated in one instance in particular that comes to mind. It would be typical for several members of the group to be in the same trades since the traders would communicate their trading ideas on a common portal. One day, their strategy picked up a trade in the NZD/CAD pair. However, they were going to make the deal on the same day that the New Zealand central bank was going to make a significant decision regarding interest rates. Given the importance of the announcement, I advised the group that it would be wiser to hold off on making an entrance into the pair until after the volatility had subsided. It didn't take me long to be reminded that XYZ traders just trade "structure" and that news has no actual impact on price direction other than to increase volatility. These folks made the trade despite my cautions, hours before the announcement. The markets reacted...wildly* when the rate was revealed. The cost suddenly dropped. By the time these traders' stops had been reached due to the volatility and speed of the markets, they were experiencing slippage in the neighborhood of 160%, which meant that transactions that had been sized for a 1% risk were being closed for a 2.6% loss. Fortunately, the majority of these traders, like me, were following a low risk per trade methodology, taking a maximum risk of 1% of the account balance per trade. Despite the fact that a 2.6% drawdown won't cause irreversible harm to an account, it's neither desirable nor essential. Understand the news.

Every week, dozens of news releases are issued. Fortunately, because many of these occurrences are low effect releases, it's not required to take them into account or even be aware of them. When entering our trades and during the anticipated lifetime of them, we need to be aware of the high-impact, market-moving news events. I want to keep the content of this book as technically oriented as possible so that the emphasis will remain on price action and market structure, but I believe it would be incompetent to simply list the news events that a trader should be aware of without providing even a cursory explanation of what they are and mean. For a list of high-impact announcements that every trader should be aware of, see below. As part of your weekend routine, which we'll go over in more detail in chapter 10, you can use this as a quick reference guide when listing the news events for the coming week.

Gross Domestic Product (GDP): The GDP is by far the most significant economic indicator, giving a picture of the state of an economy's overall health. The entire monetary value of all products and services generated by the economy during a quarter, excluding overseas activity, is generally announced on the final day of each quarter.

Choosing an interest rate. The primary drivers of currency markets around the world are interest rates. For a currency, an increase in interest rates is typically bullish, whereas a decrease is bearish.

A popular tool for monitoring and measuring inflation rates is the consumer price index (CPI). It usually comes out in the middle of the month before it. It tries to track changes in prices for a variety of consumer goods and services. Interest rate increases can be used to combat inflation if it becomes apparent and moves past a particular point.

The number of persons without jobs, or the unemployment rate. It is determined by comparing the number of people who are currently jobless but are able and eager to work to the whole workforce of the country. Based on the notion that it might result in higher interest rates, rates that are lower than anticipated are typically favorable for the underlying currency. Numerous fundamental traders view these releases, which might be a telling statistic regarding economic performance. Currency pricing and volatility can be affected by even minor changes.

Non-Farm Payroll: Indicates the change in the total number of individuals employed over the previous month, excluding those working in the farming sector. The investing community keeps a close eye on full employment because it is one of the goals of the Federal Reserve. The USD frequently strengthens and vice versa if the reading exceeds analyst expectations.

Because the US dollar is the world's reserve currency, FOMC: Federal Open Market Committee meetings are very significant. The committee meets each month to determine rates and to discuss the efficacy of the present monetary policy as well as the state of the economy. The committee consists of members who cast votes at each meeting, with "Hawkish" members supporting an increase in interest rates and "Dovish" members supporting a decrease in rates. Traders closely examine the statement made public by the committee in search of indicators of future Central Bank behavior.

Central bank speeches, releases, and conferences: In addition to managing commercial banks and ensuring currency stability through quantitative easing, central banks also have a wide range of other duties. There are eight main central banks: the US Federal Reserve, European Central Bank, Bank of England, Bank of Japan, Swiss National Bank, Bank of Canada, Reserve Bank of Australia, and Reverse Bank of New Zealand. In order to determine whether it is likely that the bank would raise or lower interest rates, forex traders frequently analyze the Chairman of the Bank's language and words. It is crucial to take into account any central bank release if the pair being traded includes the currency of the release.

Please note that these quick summaries are just meant to provide a general summary of the news events that traders should be aware of. It is not in my goal to try to provide a more thorough analysis of how they impact the general global macro-economic environment and, potentially, the movement of specific currency pairs because it is outside the scope of this book. I've made it clear throughout the entire book that I want to keep things as applicable as possible and to concentrate only on the informational content that will benefit the reader. No such advantage will result from a global macro dissertation or a thorough examination of the currency correlation coefficient.

monetary calendar

An economic calendar will become your greatest buddy as you keep track of these crucial occasions. It displays the upcoming data releases and news events that will affect the world's currency markets. Economic calendars show these occasions together with the precise release time. Depending on how likely it is to affect the markets, each event receives a grade. Red, yellow, and green are used to indicate high, moderate, and low impact events, respectively. The majority of calendars let you set a filter to just display the high-impact, red releases. The Resources section at the conclusion of the book includes a link to the one I personally use..

Forums	**Trades**	**News**	**Calendar**	**Market**	**Brokers**	**Login**	**Join**	**5:42pm** Search
Tue Oct 15	1:30am	AUD		Monetary Policy Meeting Minutes				
	9:30am	GBP		BOE Gov Carney Speaks				
	10:45pm	NZD		CPI q/q		0.7%	0.6%	0.6%
Wed Oct 16	9:30am	GBP		CPI y/y		1.7%	1.8%	1.7%
	1:30pm	CAD		CPI m/m		-0.4%	-0.3%	-0.1%
		USD		Core Retail Sales m/m		-0.1%	0.2%	0.2%
		USD		Retail Sales m/m		-0.3%	0.3%	0.6%
	2:00pm	GBP		BOE Gov Carney Speaks				
Thu Oct 17	1:30am	AUD		Employment Change		14.7K	15.3K	37.9K
		AUD		Unemployment Rate		5.2%	5.3%	5.3%
	9:30am	GBP		Retail Sales m/m		0.0%	-0.1%	-0.3%
	Day 1	EUR		EU Economic Summit				
	1:30pm	USD		Philly Fed Manufacturing Index		5.6	7.3	12.0
	4:00pm	USD		Crude Oil Inventories		9.3M	2.7M	2.9M
	9:00pm	AUD		RBA Gov Lowe Speaks				
Fri Oct 18	Day 2	EUR		EU Economic Summit				
	6:45pm	GBP		BOE Gov Carney Speaks				
Sat Oct 19	2:50pm	GBP		Parliament Brexit Vote		Pass		

Image 5.9: A calendar of economic events that highlights significant news stories affecting the currency markets. Prior to the start of the trading week, traders should take note of these announcements over the weekend. A link to this calendar can be found in the Resources section at the book's conclusion..

Trader Action Points

• • Type 1 and Type 2 entrance procedures are available. The more frequent kind 1 entry is one that starts a trade by breaking the structure or pattern. By starting a position while it is still contained within the price pattern or structure being traded utilizing candlestick reversal patterns, Type 2 trades can be viewed as reversal trades.

- • A variety of high-impact news stories can lead to irregular price changes, volatility, and wide spreads. Using an economic calendar, traders should be aware of upcoming events before entering the market.
- • Draw relevant price patterns into charts of your favorite stocks or currency pairings to observe how you could have used Type 1 and Type 2 entrances to profit from the next moves..

CHAPTER 6 – TRADE MANAGEMENT

"If you don't stay with your winners, you are not going to be able to pay for the losers." - Jack Schwager

The succession of choices we make after entering a deal is known as trade management. Both the statistical reality of the market and our personal psyche serve as the foundation for these activities. The key to effective trade management is finding a balance between the two, which includes: • Exiting losing deals at logical points.

• Trailing our stop loss as the trade develops in order to continuously lock in profit while still giving the price breathing room and the ability to hit higher profit levels.

• Using our judgment to combine our management philosophies in a method that is suitable for that particular transaction.

• Improving profitability by increasing trades when the chance arises by using scale-ins and risk pyramiding.

This chapter aims to expose you to the two primary approaches to managing open positions as well as teach you how to use your judgement and intuition to manage your trades in a way that is in line with your personal preferences. The last point—including discretion in your management approach—is a hotly discussed topic in the trading community. One of the things you'll read a lot about in trading books is how advantageous it is to have a fully automated management system. The inference is that a robotic system frees the trader from having to choose for themselves, reducing mental and emotional stress. My experience has shown me that, in contrast to blindly adhering to the same approach, trade after trade after trade, allowing some leeway in your management style produces greater outcomes and, ironically, puts less emotional burden on you.

Before learning the trading tactics described in the following chapter, you must complete this stage. This does, however, cause a minor issue with the way the material is structured. There is no "perfect" order to understand the concepts, despite the fact that I have organized the chapters in the most logical way. When you have not yet learned a collection of trades, it is challenging to teach management approaches that are unique to that trades. However, if you haven't learned the management approaches beforehand, it can be challenging to teach you the setups and the management principles related with them. Because of this, try to avoid considering this chapter as a stand-alone entity. The setups we will examine in the following chapter are directly related to the approaches used here.

Putting the First Stop

The initial stop loss's location is the first and most crucial stage in trade management. The initial stop gives us the opportunity to choose the size of our position in the trade, as discussed in chapter 4. While everything now appears rather obvious, one crucial question remains unanswered: where do we actually set these stops?

The setup being traded will define where the stop is placed, but the idea is always the same: to quit the trade when it becomes invalid. Every trade we make is predicated on the idea that, given the market's present structure and price action, there is a statistically significant chance that the price will move in the direction we want. But just as we must decide on precise criteria before entering a trade, so too must we be expressly aware of the kind of price action that will result from the trade's failure. A violation of the primary reason we entered a transaction is a more concise approach to describe a stop loss.

Consider a stock that has been consolidating following a significant impulsive surge up, trading in a range between 95 and 100 dollars. You want to profit from a probable breach of this correction because the consolidation has clearly created a Bull Flag. You decide that the trade should only be entered if the price breaks through the $100 resistance level, so you put your entry buy order at $101, which will cause you to enter the trade if there is a clear break of the level. Think about the premise of this trade as a simple exercise: The trader believes that if price successfully breaks out of this range, it has shown a sufficient degree of buying interest to accelerate the stock to the upside and resume its impulsive advance. He has identified a period of consolidation following an impulsive move to the upside. Now analyze what would need to happen for this idea to be proven false. Remember that his entry order is configured to only execute the trade if price actually breaks out of the range by reaching the $101 price level. Therefore, it stands to reason that if the price broke out of the $95–100 range as the basis for the trade, a move back inside the range would invalidate the trade because price would not have continued its impulsive move and would instead have traded back into the range from which it broke. This would give the trader a logical area in which to place his stop — at roughly $97–$99. look at 6.1 below.

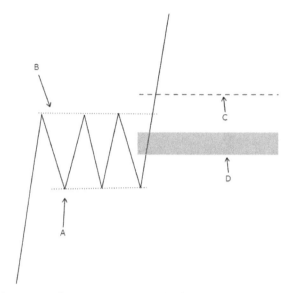

Image 6.1: placing the stop loss in a straightforward flag breakout trade. Price has stabilized in the $95 (A) to $100 (B) area. Should price successfully break out of its present range, a trade entry is placed at $101 (C). The $97-$99 range is represented by the red area at D, making this an excellent spot for the stop loss. The initial trade concept would be invalidated if price initiated the entry and then traded back inside the range to the stop level, necessitating a position exit..

We may now learn about the management techniques and the environments in which they are used by comprehending the significance of and the mechanics of stop loss placement.

1% Trailing Stop Technique

Of the two management strategies, this one is the most aggressive. It is a mechanical system that is simple to use and doesn't call for much discernment. With a predetermined 1% objective as our stop loss, this approach aggressively locks in profit as the trade goes in our favor. It works best when playing impulsive legs on the smaller time frames since it locks in quick profits in fast-moving transactions without becoming upset. The disadvantage is that these trades can frequently be abandoned when price develops greater, deeper corrections before continuing in the direction that was initially predicted. Its guidelines are straightforward: the stop loss is behind 1% for each 1% of profit the trade moves in our favor..

Image 6.2: after a straightforward Bear Flag, the 1% halt path in action. The stop loss should have been moved to 4% when the price reached the 5% profit level, but it was struck shortly after. The picture shows how the stop was trailed before it was activated.

• An easy rising structure can be seen in the illustration. The pattern's Retrace is where the trade entry is started, with the stop loss placed just above the structure.

• The exchange is carried out, and things turn out swiftly in my favor. I move my stop loss to my entry price, or the breakeven point, as soon as the price reaches the 1% profit level. My new objective is now a 2% profit goal.

• I adjust the stop loss (now at the breakeven point) to the 1% profit level as soon as the price reaches the 2% profit level. The subsequent goal is 3%.

• The stop loss is lowered to the 2% level as soon as the price reaches the 3% level.

• This process goes up until the trade is stopped out for a 4% profit.

Building Trailing Method

The second management system is a more arbitrary one that uses the market's emerging structures and patterns as our stop loss management guidelines. It is impossible to distill price action into a clear set of defined rules because of its dynamic, ever-changing nature, but take into account the following principles:

- New structures determine where to set stop losses. As these structures take shape, we hold off on adjusting the stop until price breaks them in the trade direction.
- The deal is managed according to the time frame on which it was placed. A trade entered on the 1-hour chart will utilize 1-hour structures to control the stop loss, whereas a deal conducted on the 15-minute chart would use 15-minute structures..

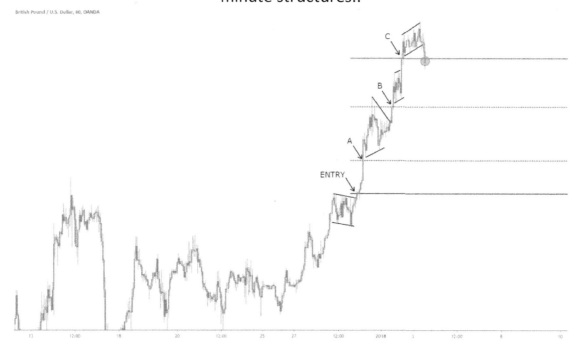

Image 6.4: The stop loss is trailed behind newly completed structures (A,B, and C) formed on the entrance time frame when using the market structure management method. The stop loss point (red circle) is activated when price breaches the structure at C..

Take Profit Orders

It makes more natural sense to let these trades run in our favor as long as possible rather than limiting our potential profit by employing profit orders because the fundamental premise of this trading method is to predict and capture the market's impulsive moves. However, there are instances when it is advantageous to exit a transaction and collect profits at predetermined targets. Profit orders are typically utilized at structural market points where it is unlikely that prices will continue to move in the desired direction. Let's examine the primary situations where employing a fixed profit target might be advantageous:

As the market reaches resistance or support

Consider that area as an excellent place to grab profits if you have found distinct HTF support and resistance levels. Why forgo active earnings by waiting for the reversal and observing price trade against us if it is likely that price will reverse at that price level? Instead, prepare an order at that level so that you can exit with the most profit when the price makes contact.

Trades in CounterPattern

Fixed take profit orders are utilized in this situation the most frequently. Consider what a CounterPattern trade really entails: you are entering a trade in the opposite direction of the movement that is expected to occur in a higher time frame. As price is confined within a higher time frame structure, you are not seeking for impulsive, prolonged directional moves in these trades; rather, you are aiming for a rapid profit. You can exit your CounterPattern trades by setting take profit targets at the tops and bottoms of these patterns, just when price starts to follow the higher time frame structure. If this is unclear, carefully think about the example that follows..

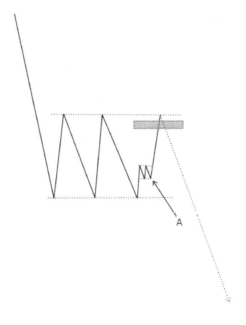

When active management is not possible

There will be instances where managing a transaction is neither realistic nor feasible. Over the next several hours or days, there will be times when you simply won't be able to check your position or alter the stop loss. For most individuals, long flights and excursions without internet or data connections don't happen frequently, yet they do. I recently visited a small town close to Marbella in Spain. A few miles from our flat, my girlfriend and I made the decision to go on a hike into the stunning mountains. Since our project took longer than we had planned, it is safe to state that we had no data service at all during that time. I had closed off a deal I had made earlier that day for breakeven when I arrived back to the apartment. I looked at the chart to see that it had been making 4% before quickly retracing to my entry price when it encountered overhead resistance. Normally, I would have exited the trade at the resistance area for a 3.7% profit, but I was unable to manage the deal and received nothing. I could have set a take profit order and exited the trade with a big profit if I had planned for the potential that I wouldn't be able to handle the deal. Take profit orders are similar to your quiet pals; they wait patiently in the market when you can't, always prepared to close a transaction and lock in profits. Use them as the occasion demands.

Discretion

All of these management techniques are effective, however individual traders may be better suited to one than another. It is the trader's responsibility to examine these strategies, putting them through a series of statistical tests to determine which ones suit his particular trading style the best. However, it is feasible to have a distinctive management approach that combines the two approaches into a personalized management strategy. Numerous trading systems are created with set management guidelines that are used consistently across all trades. These are undoubtedly legitimate strategies, and I frequently managed trades using them when I was younger and still developing. However, the majority of discretionary traders want and will tend toward an active management style that enables them to make choices based on a variety of technical and emotional factors. One of the key benefits of being a discretionary trader is that the decision of when and how to manage a trade is frequently linked to deeper issues involving the trader's situation at the time of entry.

When distinct structures have emerged, for instance, you can choose to use the fixed 1% trailing rule until those structures serve as the foundation for your stop point. Depending on the events leading up to the deal, you might even decide to make a modest alteration to your guidelines. For instance, whenever I am up on the month by 5% or more, I am always more conservative in my management approach, more keen to seize the bigger gain, and more willing to endure the deeper pullbacks and corrections. Because I've locked in healthy earnings, I feel more at ease if a 3% profit pulls back and takes me out for 1%, etc.

If you choose to use a more hybrid management style, just be aware that having a solid plan before you join a trade can lessen your tendency to act emotionally when faced with the rigors of a live market situation.

Scaling-in and Risk in Profitability Maximization Pyramiding

Trade management involves more than just understanding when to exit a position; it also involves maximizing the profits we may get from a trading idea by executing additional, multiple trade setups. In other words, effective trade management requires both understanding when to add and when to close. The two methods that follow will demonstrate how to efficiently leverage extra trade settings to increase your trading profits while maintaining your 1% risk management methodology.

Scaling-In

By adding new positions to the original transaction, scaling in enables a trader to fully profit from an irrational move. A scale-in can potentially treble the gains from the initial trade, but it comes with a cost: if the scale-in hits its 1% stop loss point, you might end up eating into the first transaction's locked-in winnings. Scale-ins should only be used in certain trading circumstances where there is a high-quality setup that is in line with the momentum of the higher time frame. Let's examine a case in point.

After the third distinct rejection at the top of an upward reversal channel, let's say you entered a Retrace trade. You entered the trade believing there would likely be an impulsive leg to the downside should the price breach the channel. Price has certainly broken through the channel, and enough profit has been made to justify lowering your stop loss to breakeven. Price has since corrected on an hourly basis, raising a blatant Bear Flag. You are free to take advantage of this second opportunity because the risk from the previous trade has been eliminated. You will have two open positions to profit from if price continues to move in the direction you first predicted, while never exposing your account to more than 1% risk.

There may even be numerous scale-ins when you are playing a much larger move and the market is particularly impulsive, giving you possibly two or more opportunities to fully capitalize on an impulsive directional move. These are the moments when you can quickly increase in percentage. I'll soon give a real-world illustration of how I employed scale-ins to extract double-digit returns in USD/CAD.

Scaling-in guidelines:

• With the stop placed at either breakeven or the profit target, the initial trade is risk-free.

- • The scale-in must be in the same direction as the initial trade and should be a distinct, high-probability trade with support from higher time frames..

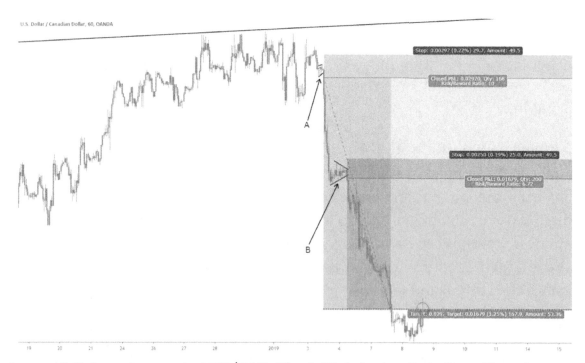

Image 6.5: Invest more in USD/CAD. The initial deal, a little Bear Flag that was placed on the 15-minute chart, is shown in Point A. Although it was not visible, the higher time period was clearly indicating that the pair may be set up for significant negative action. By the time the scale-in at B presented itself, I had

adjusted my stop to 3% profit in accordance with my management guidelines for this trade. I was free to engage any additional scale-ins because the original position was now fully risk-free. I continued using the 1% trailing strategy to manage the initial trade after B was done, setting B's stop at the same price as A. Stops for A's trade were moved to the 10% level after it reached the 11% level, and it was hit shortly after. B, the scale-in, was closed out for 6.72%, bringing the total profit from the two trades to 16.72%. Trade A was closed for a 10% profit. The duration of the post was little more than a week. The power of scaling-in is in this..

Printed in Great Britain
by Amazon

24115125R00064